Unnatural Selection

Unnatural Selection

**The Yanomami, the Kayapó
and the Onslaught of Civilisation**

Linda Rabben

**University of Washington Press
Seattle**

First published 1998 by Pluto Press
345 Archway Road, London N6 5AA

Published in the United States of America by the University of
Washington Press, PO Box 50096, Seattle WA 98145-5096

ISBN 0–295–97745–0

Designed and produced for Pluto Press by
Chase Production Services, Chadlington, OX7 3LN, England
Typeset from disk by Gawcott Typesetting, Buckingham
Printed in the EC by TJ International Ltd, Padstow

In memory of Berta G. Ribeiro, 1924–1997
Pioneira

Contents

List of Illustrations

List of Abbreviations

AVA	Associação Vida e Ambiente – Life and Environment Association
CCPY	Comissão Pró-Yanomami – Pro-Yanomami Commission
CEDI	Centro Ecumênico de Documentação e Informação – Ecumenical Center for Documentation and Information
CIMI	Conselho Indigenista Missionário – Missionary Indigenist Council
CIR	Conselho Indígena de Roraima – Indigenous Council of Roraima
FMV	Fundação Mata Virgem – Rainforest Foundation [Brazil]
FUNAI	Fundação Nacional do Índio – National Indian Foundation
IBAMA	Instituto Brasileiro do Meio-Ambiente – Brazilian Environment Institute
IDB	Inter-American Development Bank
ILRC	Indian Law Resource Center
ISA	Instituto Socioambiental – Socio-Environmental Institute
NDI	Núcleo de Direito Indígena – Indigenous Rights Unit
SPI	Serviço de Proteção aos Índios – Indian Protection Service

ix

Acknowledgements

I could not have written this book without the example and help of friends and colleagues in Brazil, the US and other countries who have dedicated themselves to defending the human rights of Brazil's most vulnerable people. Among the many who have inspired me are Claudia Andujar, Vilma Barban, Valéria de Brito, Larry Cox, Vera Fontes, Pedro Wilson Guimarães, Maria José Jaime, Michael Mary Nolan CSC, Ana de Souza Pinto, William Reinhard OMI, Fr Ricardo Rezende, Joe Rozansky OFM, Herbert de Souza (Betinho), Sr Rebecca Spires and Marcos Terena.

Organisations that assisted me in my research included the Missionary Indigenist Council (CIMI), the Pastoral Land Commission (CPT), the Pro-Yanomami Commission (CCPY), the Roraima Indigenous Council (CIR), the National Human Rights Movement (MNDH), INESC (Instituto dos Estudos Sócio-Económicos), the Socio-Environmental Institute (ISA), Survival International, the Rainforest Foundation and Amnesty International (especially the Brazil team at the International Secretariat). Rosânia Machado, Edilson Ribeiro and Jarbas Gomes Filho graciously facilitated my research in Redenção and Gorotire.

Thanks go also to the following people who consented to be interviewed: Bruce Albert, Claudia Andujar, Ana Valéria Araújo, Dr Ulisses Confalonieri, Dep. Salomão Cruz, Dr Deise Francisco, Kanyonk Kayapó, Marco Lazarin, Sérgio Leitão, Roberto Liebgott, Bishop Aldo Mongiano, Paulinho Payakan, Alcida Rita Ramos, Aurélio Rios, Dr Douglas Rodrigues, Dep. Elton Rohnelt, Márcio Santilli and Marcos Terena.

Several anthropologists have helped me tread unfamiliar ground, *quebrando o galho* (breaking the branch), as the Brazilians say. Terence Turner's dedication to indigenous people and his substantive efforts on their behalf have profoundly influenced and heartened me; he responded generously to many requests for help, advice and information. Gale Goodwin Gomez gave me the idea for the book and encouraged me along the way. Alcida Ramos, Bruce Albert, Marco Lazarin and Gilberto Azanha shared their insights about indigenous people. I am also grateful to historian Thomas Holloway of Cornell University, for reading a chapter draft. Any errors in this book are my own responsibility.

Friends have shown me great kindness. Margrit de Marez Oyens of Rio de Janeiro has offered crucial moral support over the years. Jo-Marie Griesgraber helped at a critical moment. Other friends who have provided hospitality and help include Moyra Ashford, Vilma Barban, Maria José Jaime, Jan Rocha and Alison Sutton.

Berta G. Ribeiro, to whose memory the book is dedicated, made a distinguished career in Brazil as an interpreter of indigenous material culture. She was born in Romania in 1924. After migrating to Brazil in the 1930s, she and her family experienced great hardship and political persecution. Her father was deported to Europe and died in the Holocaust. As a teenager she was left to fend for herself in São Paulo. This period was so painful to recall that 50 years later she could not bear to discuss it.

In 1948 she began working with the renowned anthropologist Darcy Ribeiro. That year she accompanied him to Kadiweu, Kaiwá and Terena villages in southern Mato Grosso. The couple did field work with the Kadiweu for about eight months. In 1951 they did research in Kaingang and Xokleng villages in Paraná and Santa Catarina.

Berta Ribeiro received a bachelor's degree in geography and history in 1953 from the then-University of the Federal District. During the 1950s she established herself as an expert in indigenous material culture at the Indian Museum and the National Museum in Rio de Janeiro. When Darcy Ribeiro moved to the new capital of Brasilia in 1958, to establish the federal university there, she went with him. The couple continued their collaboration with *The Indians and Civilisation* and *The Americas and Civilisation*.

In 1964, when a military regime took over the Brazilian government, Darcy Ribeiro was one of the first opponents to be jailed. After publication of *The Americas and Civilisation* was suspended and all copies of the book were destroyed in 1968, the couple went into exile in Uruguay, Venezuela, Chile and Peru. Berta Ribeiro returned to Brazil in 1974 and continued working on indigenous material culture. She completed her PhD in anthropology at the University of São Paulo in 1980, at age 56.

The 1980s marked the peak of her career as a researcher and teacher. She published eight books and some 50 articles, participated in innumerable working groups, seminars and congresses, did field research, worked at the Indian Museum and supervised graduate students at the Federal University of Rio de Janeiro

(UFRJ). She was named assistant professor of anthropology at UFRJ in 1988, and in 1989 she was promoted to associate professor.

In the midst of all this activity, she found time to organise the exhibition "Amazonia Urgente, Cinco Séculos de História e Ecologia" (Essential Amazon, Five Centuries of History and Ecology) and produce a 270-page guide. The exhibition opened at the Brazilian Congress in 1989. Subsequently it traveled to Salvador, Bahia, and Rio de Janeiro. During the 1992 Earth Summit, the exhibition was displayed in a subway station in downtown Rio, where thousands of people saw it.

Berta Ribeiro did field work with indigenous peoples in the Upper and Middle Xingu, Mato Grosso, Pará and the Upper Rio Negro. Her most beautiful work is the lavishly illustrated bilingual book, *Arte Indigena, Linguagem Visual/Indigenous Art, Visual Language* (1989). Her other books include *O Indio na Cultura Brasileira* (The Indian in Brazilian Culture) and *Diário do Xingu* (Xingu Diary).

Berta Ribeiro not only studied indigenous people, she collaborated with them as equals and did everything she could to defend their interests. A scrupulous and ethical scholar and a steadfast friend, she inspired the respect and deep affection of the people of many cultures who were privileged to know her.

Introduction

May 1992 – a warm and golden autumn in Brazil. For some reason, the state government of Rio de Janeiro offered the grounds of a *manicômio* – a prison farm for the criminally insane – to the organisers of the international indigenous conference. The farm is located on the periphery of Rio, not far from Riocentro, the convention center that serves as the site of the United Nations Conference on Environment and Development (UNCED), also known as the Earth Summit.

Indians from central Brazil arrived weeks ago, to build a *maloca* (communal house) of timber and palm thatch. The *maloca* is about 60 feet long, meticulously finished and very photogenic. But its entry is rather small, and only men seem to go in and out.

Across from the *maloca* is the center of conference activity, a large shelter thatched halfway down to the ground, where indigenous people from all over the world meet in formal sessions for five days. Mapuches from Chile chat with Sami from Finland; a Zuni from New Mexico gives an interview to a Brazilian journalist while a British photographer snaps Guarani dancers in elaborate feather head-dresses. Many of the sessions feature dancing, rather than talking, and some of the sessions are closed to non-indigenous people. Language is a problem, since there are not enough interpreters to go around, and electronic translation is out of the question. Perhaps that is why dancing becomes such an important part of the meetings: for many of the participants, it is the most efficient and eloquent means of communicating across linguistic and cultural barriers.

The Brazilian Indians tend not to go to the sessions for South American Indians, which are conducted in Spanish. Besides, the meeting participants are drafting written documents, and many of the Brazilian Indians are illiterate, or barely literate, in Portuguese. For them, words written on a piece of paper are not important, and spending hours arguing over phrases holds no interest. They talk quietly with one another or with non-indigenous visitors until it is time to dance.

1

Kayapó Indian records the opening of Kari-Oca
indigenous conference on video.
Photo by Cristiana Isidoro/Agência JB, May 1992.

One afternoon Davi Yanomami takes the floor. His translator announces that he and a young warrior will perform the most sacred and important of Yanomami dances, to fight evil spirits. Davi pushes powder into a thin meter-long wooden tube. The young warrior wears delicate feather decorations on his arms and ears and a red woven loincloth. At a signal from Davi he puts the end of the tube to his nose. Davi blows the powder through the tube as the young man inhales. I feel I am watching something I should not be seeing, something intimate. The crowd quiets as the young warrior dances and chants for about 20 minutes.

As he dances, a Venezuelan journalist steps into the circle and films him with a video camera, sometimes moving directly into his path, thrusting the camera into his face. His actions seem blasphemous, although the dancer, deep in trance, seems oblivious to the intruder. For a few moments we were journeying to a far-off place with the dancer, but now we are pushed back into a meaning-starved world without respect or compunction, the world some of us traveled thousands of miles to escape. The audience gasps, then mutters resentfully, but the warrior keeps dancing. He is confronting the enemies of us all.

At the end of the gathering, some of the participants produce a one-page declaration in English, Spanish and Portuguese that reaffirms indigenous demands for basic human rights, especially land rights. It is presented to the press and, perhaps, to some of the government delegates at the Riocentro. More important is the gathering itself, a manifestation of indigenous solidarity that defines what the diverse participants have in common: their identity as the original inhabitants of whatever land they come from; their denunciation of the terrible persecutions they have suffered for their differentness; their connection with what those estranged from nature call nature; and their insistence on enduring.

A few days later, Paulinho Payakan's face appears on the cover of Brazil's leading news magazine. Above the painful close-up of his unsmiling face is a bright red headline: "The Savage." Payakan has been accused of raping a young white woman in the frontier town of Redenção, Pará. That night on nationwide television, Payakan sheepishly says, "I did it, but I can't remember because I was drunk." Is it coincidental that this story appears on the day the Earth Summit begins?

Despite the fact that I have met Payakan, Davi and many other Brazilian Indians and followed their stories, I am an outsider to all this. A middle-class kid from Philadelphia, I became an anthropologist but did not study Indians. Instead I did research on urban elites. After almost two years' field research in Rio in 1978–9, I kept returning to the big cities, captivated by the community move-ments that were trying to transform Brazil. The Brazil I came to know was not beaches, carnival and *futebol* but a darker world of social and economic injustice on a massive scale – and the deter-mined people who were fighting it.

By the mid-1980s I realised that to understand urban Brazil, I had to understand rural Brazil. My travels took me to daub-and-wattle shacks in the Northeastern backlands, burgeoning slums in the Amazon and the union headquarters in Xapuri, Acre, where Chico Mendes waged his fatal battle on behalf of the rubber tappers and the forests that provided their sustenance.

Back in Washington, DC, I met indigenous leaders who were traveling the world to call attention to the situation of their people in Brazil. The hot summers of 1987 and 1988 spurred international concern about Amazon deforestation as a contributor to global warming. Politically canny environmentalists touted the Indians as protectors of the rainforests. Meanwhile, coalitions of non-governmental organisations (NGOs) pressured Northern govern-ments and banks to stop lending money to Brazil and other devel-oping countries for environmentally destructive "mega-projects."

Early in 1988 Paulinho Payakan came to Washington for the first time, to denounce Brazilian hydroelectric projects that, if funded by the World Bank, would flood the homeland of his people, the Kayapó. Later that year, on a trip to Belém, at the mouth of the Amazon, I met Payakan and Darrell Posey, an American anthropologist then living in Brazil. Payakan seemed guarded, uncomfortable, suspicious. The normally ebullient Posey suddenly found himself in a great deal of trouble after accompa-nying two Kayapó to the US and translating for them when they visited the World Bank. Along with Payakan and another young Kayapó leader, he was indicted under the Brazilian Foreigners Law, a grim relic of the military dictatorship. After an international campaign, the charges were dropped, but Posey's life changed greatly. He left his job in Brazil and went on to Oxford University, to do research on the more general issue of intellectual property rights for indigenous peoples.

I wrote an article about Posey's troubles for the American Anthropological Association's newsletter and other articles about what was going on in Brazil for the publication of the Brazil Network, a small NGO I coordinated for almost three years. Through all these activities I became familiar with the Brazil of land conflicts, death squads and environmental devastation.

The Brazilian activists I encountered kept asking, "If you go home and write about us, what good will that do us?" One can never be sure what effect one's work will have. But it is clear that hundreds of books, articles, Urgent Action Appeals and other documents published during the past decade have helped Brazil's indigenous people in their struggle to survive and preserve their traditional ways of life. The resulting international attention and pressure have made a positive difference to the Kayapó, the Yanomami and other groups.

Nobody has expressed this more eloquently than Davi Yanomami, who has traveled the world on behalf of his people. In Rio in 1992, he told film-maker Geoffrey O'Connor:

> People a long way from here hear what we say and support us. They really support us. You people here [filming] are also helping us. If we weren't supported like this, we would think, "Are we going to die?" That's what we wonder: "Are we all going to disappear?" And a lot of white people take our words round the world. Many people heard these words; they became well known. The Brazilian government tried to hide us, but they can't do that anymore; our words are known everywhere. Help from the white world is important to us. (CCPY 1993: 18)

In October 1990 I went to London to work as a researcher for Amnesty International. For a year I toiled over the files of Brazil's threatened, the tortured, the killed and the "disappeared." Working for Amnesty made me feel not only useful but accepted by the Brazilian activists I admired. As a result I met and collaborated with people to whom I had had no access before.

In the late 1980s, after traveling round the world with Raoni, a charismatic indigenous leader, the British rock star Sting had started the Rainforest Foundation to fulfill his promises to Raoni's people, the Kayapó of central Brazil. At the invitation of the Foundation's director, who had worked for Amnesty International, I joined the Foundation in October 1991. For the first time in my career I was working on indigenous issues and in frequent contact with indigenous people. The few Brazilian Indians I had met before were world travelers, and we met in New York, London, Brasilia or Washington. Some had spent many years in cities and were far from their places and cultures of origin. Their constituencies were other indigenous leaders, professional activists and supporting intellectuals, in Brazil and beyond.

During my year at the Rainforest Foundation, I met Indians who still lived in reserves and traveled only rarely to the city. In preparing for UNCED, I read a great deal about the Kayapó and other Brazilian indigenous groups, met prominent Kayapó including Raoni and Payakan, and learned about the international indigenous movement. As a result of these experiences, I came to appreciate how ingeniously and persistently indigenous people strive to protect and preserve their culture in the face of great obstacles and dangers. And I started to work on this book.

In 1993 I visited an indigenous reserve in the Western Amazon as an Amnesty International volunteer. The journey seemed long and complicated, though nothing compared to the marathon treks of some anthropologists: a plane from Manaus to the frontier town of Tabatinga, a 45-minute motorboat ride over the unexpectedly rough waters of the Solimões (Upper Amazon) River to the town of Benjamin Constant, another boat ride on the Javari River to the Ticuna reserve, and long walks along slippery tree trunks and muddy paths to four Ticuna villages. There I visited the survivors of a March 1988 massacre, allegedly committed by the hired guns of a Brazilian logger greedy for Ticuna land, in which 14 Ticuna, including several children, were killed. Almost ten years later, those responsible had not yet been brought to justice.

The Ticuna were hospitable and kind, but communication was difficult. The widows and mothers of the massacre victims did not speak Portuguese, so my Ticuna hosts (who lived in town) interpreted. Each time I met one of the survivors, I shook her hand; each survivor giggled, whether out of embarrassment or amusement I could not tell.

After a long day of visits and walks between villages, we returned to Benjamin Constant. The leading news story on television that night was the massacre of 16 Yanomami on Brazil's frontier with Venezuela. At five the next morning I telephoned Amnesty in London with the news. "Oh, we already know about that," the researcher said. "CNN called for our comment."

The massacre had happened about six weeks earlier, and it had taken all that time for the report to reach the outside world, via a letter from a Brazilian nurse who lived and worked in Yanomami territory. The Minister of Justice had thought it important enough to make the announcement himself on nationwide television – quite a contrast with earlier government reaction (or lack thereof) to the plight of the Yanomami. The ensuing flurry of government activity resulted from constant international pressure on behalf of the Yanomami over several years. In the case of the Ticuna and scores of other indigenous groups, however, international attention has been sporadic or transitory. Consequently, most of Brazil's 300,000 indigenous people live in a state of silent deprivation. When they do call for help, few hear them.

The subjects of this book, the Kayapó and Yanomami, have become emblematic figures for millions of people throughout the world. Thanks to Sting's efforts, the Kayapó leader Raoni became internationally famous in the late 1980s, along with his kinsman Payakan. A skilled organiser, Payakan arranged the famous indigenous meeting at Altamira in 1989. His career as an activist goes back to the early 1980s. The Yanomami are well known to hundreds of thousands of college graduates who have read Napoleon Chagnon's book, *The Fierce People*, as an assigned text in anthropology courses since the late 1960s. In recent years Davi Yanomami has journeyed to North America and Europe to call for action to save his people, whose plight became generally known after 40,000 gold miners invaded their lands in the late 1980s. Many other indigenous groups in Brazil face similar threats to their cultural and physical survival, but the Kayapó and the Yanomami have gained the world's attention. I try to show how and why in this book.

Many anthropologists and other scholars have spent their careers studying indigenous people in Brazil and other countries. Without their work, the rest of us would know almost nothing about these groups, which might have disappeared without notice. The information and interpretations the anthropologists make available to the world undoubtedly help indigenous people in their struggle to survive and prosper. In researching this book, I have had the benefit of reading their articles and books, which have strongly influenced me, and of talking with them about their experiences and ideas.

Some of these scholars have become activists because of their sense of personal commitment to the people they study. They have moved from the classroom and the library to the arenas of political and economic power. Their dedication to both knowledge and action has inspired me. For example, Terence Turner (University of Chicago) has studied the Kayapó for more than 30 years and has helped them become video chroniclers of their culture and history. Bruce Albert (French Institute of Scientific Research for Development in Cooperation) found the survivors of the 1993 Yanomami massacre and recorded their account of the killings. At some personal risk, Alcida Ramos (University of

Brasilia) has delivered emergency medical aid to the Yanomami. She and Kenneth Taylor, a British anthropologist, developed the first plan to create a Yanomami reserve in the early 1970s. Darrell Posey risked his career to help the Kayapó gain international attention for their opposition to hydroelectric projects. Many others have given various kinds of material help. Some have testified as expert witnesses before Congressional or parliamentary committees in the US, Brazil and Europe. Still others continue to gather, interpret and publish information about indigenous people despite great practical and political difficulties. Their efforts reinforce the work of non-anthropologists, such as Claudia Andujar, who have dedicated themselves to defending indigenous interests. Often the indigenous activists who visit us seem to stand alone against an uncomprehending and hostile world. But they could not reach us to convey their messages without the support of people like these, who share their concerns and their determination. They, too, are part of the story.

This book is neither a traditional ethnography, based on prolonged field research in an indigenous community, nor a theoretical work. It is, rather, a piece of applied anthropology that draws on a wide variety of primary and secondary sources. The extensive ethnographic literature about the Kayapó and Yanomami has provided a great deal of detailed information that I have used to chronicle the history of the two groups. I have also consulted books, films and articles on development in the Amazon and other regions of Brazil, human rights reports from international organisations such as Amnesty International, Internet postings from indigenous and solidarity organisations in Brazil and other countries, and my own notes on more than a decade's work with Brazilian grassroots movements. Rather than focus narrowly on the Kayapó and Yanomami, as if they were self-contained, untouched cultures, I seek to show their inevitable, crucial connections to the surrounding society and the rest of the world.

In this book I use the terms "North" and "South" to discuss developed and developing countries. "First World" and "Third World" lost their currency and usefulness with the end of the Cold War (and the disappearance of the "Second World"). The "civilisation" in the book's subtitle is the result of two millennia of colonisation, imperialism and globalisation – a world economic, social and political system that links accountants in Tokyo, aborigines in the Australian outback, mahogany trees in the Brazilian Amazon and mountain gorillas in Rwanda in a complex network of ideas, beliefs, hardware, software, weapons of mass destruction and millions of other material objects. This civilisation is not exactly western or eastern but has pretensions to universality.

To set the scene, Chapter 1 surveys the dizzying changes that civilisation has brought to the Amazon region. Road building, mining, ranching, logging, colonisation, hydroelectric projects, deforestation, urban development – all have come to the Amazon in a rush, and the results have overwhelmed both the environment and its traditional inhabitants. The region's indigenous people have become symbols of the most ancient ways of living in and with nature, even as they struggle to cope with and adjust to the modern world.

Our understanding of indigenous people (not to mention their understanding of us) is rooted in 500 years of tumultuous history. Chapter 2 examines some of the most important accounts – from the first description of indigenous Brazilians in 1500 to scholarly interpretations of the 1990s – that have defined them for the outside world.

The Kayapó have been in contact with outsiders for hundreds of years. Chapter 3 recounts the history of their struggle to survive civilisation. Their persistence in preserving their traditional culture, their warlike behavior, their colorful appearance and their political exploits have made them especially visible. Their deals with gold miners, which made them wealthy, also had serious negative consequences, including mercury contamination of their land, air and water. As the richest indigenous group in Brazil, the Kayapó now stand at a crossroads, as they try to decide what kind of development will benefit them most.

Chapter 4 recounts the rise and fall of the Kayapó leader Payakan, who first came into contact with whites as a teenage worker on a road building crew in the Amazon. Throughout the 1980s he led young warriors in symbolic confrontations with the Brazilian government. As a result of the deals he and other leaders helped broker, the Kayapó became Brazil's richest indigenous group. In the process he became famous. His career as an international figure crashed in 1992, when he was accused of rape. Although the charges against him were dismissed two years later, he has not regained his former status. Sadly, Payakan's trajectory is not uncommon among indigenous people who become defenders of their people.

The Yanomami, whose history is recounted in Chapter 5, are best known as "the fierce people," the title of Napoleon Chagnon's famous ethnography. Despite their ferocity, they have become victims of disease, invasion and exploitation. Although they are often described as the largest uncontacted indigenous group in South America, scholarly research shows that they have been in indirect contact with the outside world for a very long time. Overwhelming contact began in the mid- and late 1980s, when 40,000 gold miners (twice the Yanomami's total number in Brazil and Venezuela) invaded their territory. Some 20 per cent of the Yanomami may have died of disease or as a result of violent conflicts with miners since 1987. The worst incident was the July 1993 Haximu massacre, when Brazilian miners allegedly killed 16 Yanomami men, women and children just over the Venezuelan border. Unlike the Kayapó, the Yanomami's prospects are not good.

In contrast to Payakan stands another indigenous leader, Davi Yanomami, the subject of Chapter 6, who has become famous through his international tours. Davi is a shaman who speaks simply but powerfully in prophecies, myths and oracles. His poetic predictions of doom have a hypnotic effect on audiences worried about environmental degradation. Supporting Davi are Brazilian and other anthropologists, medical professionals and activists who lobbied and worked for a Yanomami reserve in northern Brazil for more than 20 years.

Although similar in many respects, the histories of the Kayapó and Yanomami differ in important ways that may determine their destinies. Both are part of a much larger struggle for cultural and physical survival. The final chapter looks at the evolutionary prospects of indigenous peoples and our species in general.

A final note: indigenous people continue to seek outside help in defending their cultures, territories, rights and interests. In association with environmental and human rights organisations, they have taken to the Internet to inform the global public about their struggle to survive. Readers who want to help can find information about indigenous activism and appeals for solidarity in many sites on the World Wide Web.

1

Setting the Scene

During the past decade, the Kayapó and the Yanomami have become the most famous of almost 200 indigenous groups in Brazil. Painted, befeathered and armed with stout clubs, the Kayapó have strutted across the world stage, while the Yanomami have been portrayed as once-proud savages reduced to helpless victims of white men's greed. Why and how did these two groups gain the world's attention? To understand, we need to see them in historical, political and economic context.

Modernisation, Military Style

In 1964 a military regime took over Brazil after more than a decade of elected civilian government. Armed with a modernising, authoritarian, anticommunist ideology, the military tried to transform Brazil from a predominantly rural country dominated by big landowners exporting natural resources into an industrialised, urbanised world power. They partly succeeded. In 1950, 70 per cent of Brazil's population lived in the countryside; in 1985, when the military retired to the barracks, 70 per cent lived in urban areas. By that time Brazil boasted the world's eighth largest industrial economy (and the developing world's largest international debt). At the end of the twentieth century, Brazil exported steel, airplanes, automobile engines, precision tools and shoes, as well as the traditional agricultural commodities, coffee and sugar. But social scientists classified more than half of its 160 million people as poor or indigent; the richest 10 per cent of the population held 45 per cent of the country's income, while the poorest 50 per cent held less than 2 per cent of income (Roque *et al.* n.d.: 1).

> Despite the economic growth of the past half-century, two-thirds of the population live below the officially defined poverty level of roughly $200 a month ... According to a 1995 World Bank study, Brazil has the most unequal distribution of

11

wealth of any country in the world. Brazil remains a rich country full of poor people. (Eakin 1997: 5)

From the 1960s on, Brazil's generals and technocrats were determined to develop the vast interior. In their mind's eye they saw endless soybean fields, thousands of grazing cattle, sugar mills, light industry, burgeoning towns, highways, dams, mines and tree plantations – a panorama as prosperous and civilised as the US Middle West. The reality was very different: interminable, impenetrable rainforests, a handful of unpaved roads, hundreds of unnav-

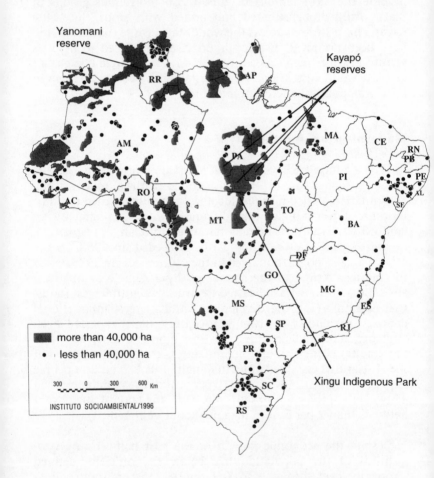

Map of indigenous territories in Brazil.
Ricardo and Santilli 1996, courtesy of Instituto Socioambiental.

igable rivers, a few thousand backwoodsmen and their families clinging to the shores, a few thousand Indians living in the woods.

After 1964 the military persuaded the World Bank, the Inter-American Development Bank, Northern governments, corporations and banks to support their ambitious development plans. The Brazilian government then offered generous subsidies to domestic and foreign companies to open up the Amazon, created hundreds of state-controlled enterprises, built giant hydroelectric projects and interstate highways in the remotest parts of the country, and sent hundreds of thousands of migrants to settle along the roads. One of the military rulers touted the project as "a land without men for men without land."

The Indigenous Presence

But Brazil's interior was not empty. The Kayapó, the Yanomami and many other indigenous groups already lived there. The Yanomami had little direct contact with outsiders, but the Kayapó had been dealing and warring with Brazilians for more than a hundred years. When roads reached both groups in the late 1960s, Davi Yanomami and Paulinho Payakan, both of whom later became internationally famous, went to work on the construction crews. Thus they had their first sustained contact with Brazilians, improved the Portuguese they had learned from missionaries, and picked up the rudiments of Brazilian culture. The roads also brought disease, prostitution, malnutrition, environmental degradation, crime and a host of other ills to the Indians. They had to learn quickly how to cope, or die.

Many did die. Davi Yanomami's mother succumbed to disease brought to her village by missionaries. Often, half of "pacified" Indian villages would die in epidemics soon after contact with Brazilians. "Hostile" groups, like the Kayapó, had a better survival rate. Nonetheless, the entire Kayapó population decreased from around 4,000 in 1900 to about 1,500 in 1960. By 1990 their numbers had gone back up to 4,000.

Through a series of dramatic struggles with Brazilians, the Kayapó found ways to survive and prosper. The more numerous Yanomami have experienced genocide and also survived, but it remains to be seen if they will manage to preserve their identity and traditional way of life. Many other indigenous groups have not survived, either physically or culturally. Decimated, pushed off their land or surrounded by impinging outsiders, they migrated to urban slums or faded into the miserable "rural proletariat."

Development for Some

The development of Brazil's interior has been apparently chaotic, with violent conflicts over land, guerrilla warfare, assassinations of peasant leaders by hired gunmen, large-scale devastation of virgin forests by settlers, loggers and miners, uncontrolled urban growth and outbreaks of contagious diseases. The most famous example of developmental disaster is the Polonoroeste Project, funded by the World Bank in the early 1980s, when hundreds of thousands of migrants went to the frontier state of Rondonia and cut or burned three-quarters of its forests. After cultivating crops that exhausted the soil along the highways, they moved deeper into the forests, repeating the same disastrous pattern of slashing and burning. This kind of swidden agriculture may work on a small scale, but not when thousands of people do it on hundreds of thousands of acres of deforested soil unsuited to cultivation.

Across the Amazon, ranching, mining and logging have had massively destructive effects. Both the Kayapó and the Yanomami have confronted thousands of wildcat gold miners (*garimpeiros*) who have invaded their territories. As many as 300,000 garimpeiros are said to be wandering through the Amazon region, living and working in miserable conditions. They pan for gold, blasting out riverbanks with high-pressure hoses and separating out the gold with highly toxic mercury. The consequences include deforestation, erosion, flooding, violence, malaria and other diseases, and mercury contamination of soil, water, air and the food chain (MacMillan 1995).

Logging, mining and ranching destroy biodiversity, ruin the land for traditional uses, and cause conflicts inside indigenous groups as some leaders sell off resources while others resist such deal making. These conflicts divide groups at the very moment when they need to unite if they are to protect themselves and their way of life from outside threats to their cultural and physical integrity.

Though apparently chaotic, this kind of "development" does have an internal logic. In the short term, the few who take big risks to invest capital can reap big rewards. Those with economic, political and social power have a tremendous advantage over the powerless. Force, impunity, fraud and corruption flourish. Long-term consequences seem irrelevant, though eventually the crash must come. In a larger sense, it seems as if nothing ever changes: the rich win, the poor lose, at a terrible cost in resources and lives. This "boom–bust cycle" has recurred throughout Brazil's history. It explains the coexistence of elaborate palaces and wretched hovels on the same frontier streets, in towns where only 10 per cent of the population has electricity, drinkable water or sewage pipes.

The military wanted to break the boom–bust cycle and establish permanent development in the interior by building infrastructure, settling thousands on the land, cultivating vast areas and establishing urban centers. Unlike the US midwestern prairie, however, much of the Amazon's soil is not fertile enough to feed millions. The costs of bringing electricity and natural gas to its cities are high. Severe environmental damage and disappointing outcomes have made ambitious "mega-projects" very risky in the long term.

International Intervention

This kind of capital-intensive development requires outside support. The nationalistic military had an ambivalent relationship with international backers, who wanted a certain amount of control over the way their loans were spent. For example, in the early 1980s the Inter-American Development Bank (IDB) placed conditions on an Amazon road building project that included protection of indigenous groups living near the highway. When the military failed to comply, the IDB withdrew its funding under pressure from environmental organisations that were monitoring the project. Meanwhile, international human rights organisations kept denouncing military repression, which included torture, arbitrary imprisonment, extrajudicial executions and disappearances in the cities and the countryside.

After the dictatorship ended and as Brazil struggled to pay the interest on its enormous foreign debt, international organisations effectively pressured the World Bank to institute environmental protection policies. International solidarity groups supported Chico Mendes in his crusade to protect Brazil's rainforests and the rubber tappers who lived and worked in them.

Brazilian nationalists inside and outside the government resisted these pressures. As the Cold War waned, they abandoned the military's anticommunist rhetoric to accuse Northern governments and non-governmental organisations of conspiring, for economic reasons, to prevent Brazil from becoming a world power. There were secret plans, they claimed, for the United Nations to invade the Amazon under cover of protecting the Yanomami Indians from genocide. The foreigners were plotting to set up a puppet Yanomami state on the northern borders.

"Internationalisation of the Amazon" became the nationalists' battle cry. A report by Brazil's Superior War College in the late 1980s named environmentalists, anthropologists and missionaries as threats to national security.

When the military left power in 1985, it tried to ensure its control over Amazonia through an ambitious program called *Calha Norte* (northern headwaters), which would "Brazilianise" a 6,500-kilometer-long, 150-kilometer-wide strip along its northern borders with five countries (Rabben 1990). Troops would be based near the border, and migrants would be encouraged to settle there. A few million dollars were secretly budgeted to start up the program; troops were stationed in Yanomami territory. The 1992 demarcation of the Yanomami reserve seems to have forestalled large-scale agricultural development of the remote, mountainous area, but in 1997 the Brazilian and Venezuelan governments signed agreements to build highways and develop hydroelectric projects near the reserve. Also in the mid-1990s, Asian logging companies started buying Brazilian firms and millions of acres of forest in the Amazon. Despite government conservation measures, the rate of deforestation in Brazil increased significantly after the 1992 Earth Summit. The Environmental Defense Fund reported that forest burning increased by 50 per cent from 1996 to 1997 (Schwartzman 1997).

As a result of many years of pressure and criticism by international environmental and human rights organisations allied with local activists, the World Bank and other multilateral development institutions now hesitate to directly lend Brazil the billions of dollars necessary to bring such projects to fruition. The Brazilian government is seeking investment from corporations and private banks and is making agreements with neighboring countries to build projects that have been on the drawing board for decades. These projects may never materialise. Both international and local groups that defend the interests of Indians, other "traditional populations" and the environment are mobilising to prevent them from proceeding.

Indians in the Way

The Kayapó and the Yanomami have played central roles in the fight to stop what Brazilian officials once called "the march of progress." In the 1970s Kayapó warriors patrolled the borders of their territory with shortwave radios and did not hesitate to attack (and sometimes kill) invaders. When the Brazilian military tried to dump nuclear waste near Kayapó territory in the mid-1980s, the Indians reacted strongly and made national headlines; the military backed down. In a series of highly publicised struggles involving "ritualised warfare" with federal officials, violent actions against non-indigenous invaders and strategic alliances with sympathetic outsiders, the Kayapó became nationally and internationally known as determined, fearless, intimidating defenders of their own interests. Over the years they have acquired considerable economic and political clout, so that the Brazilian government cannot ignore their wishes as it plans the development of their region. Few other indigenous groups have managed to play such a forceful and effective role, though many also face invasion, destruction of their habitat, health problems caused by contact, lack of access to social services and other serious problems.

Preoccupied by inter-village disputes, the Yanomami were no match for invading hordes of goldminers armed with guns, air-planes and killer diseases. They have survived attempted genocide with the help of concerned outsiders, from Brazilian anthropologists to local environmental and human rights groups in New Jersey, Switzerland, Japan and many other places. Their defenders struggle to keep the Yanomami in the world spotlight and find support from international donors for projects to protect their health and educate their children.

Despite all the pressure from outsiders, however, the Brazilian government has failed to stop garimpeiros from re-entering Yanomami and other indigenous territories in numbers large enough to pose a threat to the Indians. In 1997, the Pro-Yanomami Commission (CCPY), a non-governmental organisation, estimated that 3,000 miners were still working in the Yanomami reserve. Allegedly, more miners entered the reserve during the year, after reading newspaper reports that the Congress was about to pass legislation opening indigenous areas to mineral exploration (*Folha de Boa Vista* 1997). The $6 million that the Congress had appropriated to expel the miners in 1996 were not used until November 1997 (CCPY 1997 *Update*, CIMI 1997d). Almost 400 Federal Police, army, air force, FUNAI and IBAMA agents expelled only a few hundred miners and temporarily blocked 30 airstrips inside the Yanomami reserve. It remains to be seen if this operation will have any more long-term effect than previous ones.

Meanwhile, the Brazilian government has to cope with constant pressure from the "Amazon bloc," Congress members from the Amazon states who defend the kind of development that makes Indians disappear. Responding to political pressure, in early 1996 the Justice Minister promulgated new regulations making it possible for state governments and private interests to challenge the demarcation of indigenous reserves, even when signed by the President – as long as the demarcation had not been registered at the local land office.[1] More than 1,000 challenges were filed at FUNAI, the Indian protection agency, and not one was upheld. Later, however, the Justice Minister used the decree to question eight controversial demarcations. Just before he left office in early 1997, he ordered one of these, the Raposa/Serra do Sol reserve (next to the Yanomami reserve in the border state of Roraima) to be reduced in size by about 20 per cent.

Indigenous advocates believe this "Decree 1775/96" was a response to demands from the Amazon bloc to roll back demarcations that threatened powerful regional interests' development plans. In 1997, a Brazilian Congress member claimed that the reduction of the Raposa/Serra do Sol reserve was part of a deal between the Justice Minister and Amazon bloc Congress members, in exchange for votes to change the Constitution to allow the re-election of Brazil's President (SEJUP 1997b).

Throughout 1996, international and Brazilian indigenous organisations protested loudly against Decree 1775/96. Amnesty International expressed concern that the decree was putting the safety of many indigenous communities at risk. After the European Parliament passed a resolution criticising the decree, Brazil's Justice Minister traveled to Europe (especially to Germany, which is funding demarcation of scores of Brazilian indigenous reserves) to explain the policy. Reaction from the US government was muted, but the US Congressional Human Rights Caucus sent a letter questioning the decree to Brazil's President. As of late 1997, the decree continued in force, slowing or stopping demarcations and creating uncertainty in indigenous communities. Around the country, tension between Indians and outsiders seemed to intensify. The Missionary Indigenist Council (CIMI) reported that invasions of indigenous areas by miners and others increased by 95 per cent in 1997, and reported disease cases by 92 per cent, over the previous year (InterPress Service 1997c).

Other indigenous groups besides the Kayapó and Yanomami have moved to center-stage in the mid-1990s. Crises have erupted among the Guarani-Kaiowá of Mato Grosso do Sul, the Pataxó of Bahia, the Krikati of Maranhão, the Nambikwara of Rondônia, all of whom feel threatened by the slowdown and uncertainty caused by Decree 1775/96. All fear violence by outsiders greedy for their land. In contrast, two of the Kayapó's three reserves are securely demarcated and cannot be challenged; the Yanomami reserve is also securely demarcated (though not safe from invasion and depredation).[2] Although their problems may seem less dramatic and therefore gain less attention than they used to, the Kayapó and Yanomami find them no less pressing. Other indigenous groups will be influenced by the strategies these two groups use to survive.

Indigenous organisations are proliferating in Brazil as Indians acquire greater knowledge of how the society works. They range from village associations to national solidarity organisations. For years Kayapó leaders from widely separated villages have been meeting whenever necessary to plan strategy, and some Kayapó communities have set up associations for sustainable development. Yanomami leaders from across their vast territory began meeting only recently. They rely on the assistance of CCPY, a 20-year-old group of Brazilian anthropologists and advocates, and the leadership of Davi Yanomami, who is trying to prepare others to follow his example. In these and other ways indigenous people are taking on the task of protecting their interests vis-à-vis the larger society. Because of their small numbers and their lack of political and economic power, they will continue to need the support of sympathetic and concerned outsiders from Brazil and beyond.

The Kayapó and the Yanomami may not be "typical," but they have come to stand for Brazilian Indians and other threatened indigenous groups around the world. To understand what they have accomplished, what problems they confront and what kind of help they seek, we will look more closely at their histories, the contrasting stories of two men who have represented them, their allies and, finally, their prospects.

2

In Search of the Other

Brazil's 500-year history of contact with Europeans begins with an encounter on a beach, far from the homelands of the Kayapó and the Yanomami. On 24 April 1500, Portuguese mariners landed on Brazil's northeastern coast and met a group of 18 to 20 men on the shore. In a letter to the King of Portugal, Pero Vaz de Caminha described them as:

> ... reddish brown, with good faces and noses, well made. They go naked, with no covering, and they make no effort either to conceal or display their shameful parts; and they go about this with as much innocence as they have in showing their faces. (Caminha 1974: 8)[1]

Caminha provided a detailed description of the Indians' decorations, hairstyle and manners. Most significant:

> One of them laid eyes on the captain's gold chain, and began pointing to the earth and then to the chain, as if to tell us that there was gold in the earth. He also saw a silver candlestick and likewise pointed to the earth and then to the candlestick, as if they also had silver. (Caminha 1974: 9)

The Portuguese saw what they wanted to see in the Indians' behavior.

Their first conclusion was that the Indians would easily be converted to Christianity "because these people are good and of good simplicity ... and He who brought us here, I believe, did not do so for no reason" (Caminha 1974: 10). Soon after this encounter, the Portuguese planted a cross on the shore and named the newfound land "The Island of the True Cross."

Later, the colony was renamed "Brasil," after the red dyewood that became its first principal export commodity. Gold and silver would not be discovered in quantity for another 200 years. Most of the Indians died before they could be converted, and the Portuguese did not take long to change their mind about their character. To the hardbitten adventurers who plunged into Brazil's uncharted interior, Indians were "good" for slavery, death or rape.

Early European encounters with indigenous people raised serious questions. Were the Indians descended from Adam? Were they really human beings? Pope Paul III declared that they were human in 1537, opening America to evangelisation. Which of Noah's sons was their ancestor, then? Were they, like the sons of Ham, destined for slavery? European invaders operated on this assumption.[2]

Portugal, France, Spain and the Netherlands fought for control of Brazil, and they often used rival indigenous groups to fight their battles. In the 1550s, the French established a colony at what is now Rio de Janeiro and invited Huguenot missionaries to live and minister there. Jean de Léry, a Calvinist preacher, spent about two years in "Antarctic France" with the Indians before returning to Europe.

Léry's Ethnography

Léry later survived the horrors of religious war in France, which included Protestants and Catholics tearing each others' hearts out and eating them. Almost 20 years after his stay in Brazil, he published *History of a Voyage to the Land of Brazil, Otherwise Called America*. His account made the allegedly cannibalistic Indians seem charming, compared to the savage Europeans. It became one of the most important sources of information about Brazilian indigenous people, along with chronicles by the French Abbé Thévet and the German mercenary Hans Staden. Even twentieth-century anthropologists like Claude Lévi-Strauss have cited Léry.

In rich and shocking detail, Léry described Tupinambá Indians ritually killing, cooking and eating their enemies, but he was most concerned to portray them as human beings with both good and bad qualities. He frequently used the Indians for moralising purposes, contrasting their virtues with the evils of Europeans, or fulminating against their lack of true religion. He also took pains to describe their physical characteristics, food, customs and religion, and to correct errors about them that were circulating in Europe. His scrupulous account can be seen as an early example of ethnography, in contrast to popular, fanciful tales of the marvels, monsters and Arcadian innocence of the "Brave New World."

The Tupinambá, he says, live long because they don't worry about the "things of this world." They don't "drink of those murky, pestilential springs, from which flow so many streams of mistrust, avarice, litigation and squabbles, of envy and ambition, which eat away our bones, suck out our marrow, waste our bodies, and consume our spirits" (Léry 1990: 57).

He admired the Indians because they were valorous, generous and virtuous.

> I have observed among them that just as they love those who are gay, joyful and liberal, on the contrary they so hate those who are taciturn, stingy and melancholy, that I can assure any who are sly, malicious, gloomy, niggardly, or who munch their bread alone in a corner, that they will never be welcome among our Tupinambá; for by their nature they detest such manner of folk. (Léry 1990: 99)

Léry professed to miss the Indians, and he clearly liked them: "Even now it seems to me that I have them before my eyes, and I will forever have the idea and image of them in my mind" (1990: 67). Recounting a pre-battle ritual, he says, "They sang so beautifully that I stood there transported with delight. Whenever I remember it, my heart trembles, and it seems their voices are still in my ears" (1990: 144). An admirer of martial valor, he reports, "I have never taken so much pleasure ... as I delighted then in seeing those savages do battle" (1990: 118).

On the other hand, Léry condemned the Tupinambá for not accepting Christianity. "When men do not recognise their Creator, it is a result of their own wickedness," he says sternly. In his eyes, the Indians were responsible for their own salvation or damnation, and he even called them "a people accursed and abandoned by God." But he persisted in believing that the Indians were "teachable."

While condemning polygamy, he admired co-wives' lack of jealousy. He praised their willingness to nurse their babies, instead of sending them to wet-nurses as French women did.

Léry never missed a chance to use the Indians to censure French failings. He mentions the generosity of Indian hosts and adds, "The hypocritical welcome of those over here who use only slippery speech for consolation of the afflicted is a far cry from the humanity of these people, whom nonetheless we call 'barbarians'" (1990: 168).

In recent years anthropologists have argued over the reliability of Léry's and others' accounts of ritual cannibalism among the Tupinambá and other Brazilian indigenous groups; some have questioned the very existence of cannibalism in the New World. Considering Léry's scrupulousness, however, it seems unlikely that he invented his account, which Thévet and Staden independently confirmed. Twentieth-century anthropologists have described other indigenous customs reported by the chroniclers that (unlike cannibalism) have survived until recent times among some groups. One example is the "welcome of tears," which Charles Wagley used as the title of his 1973 book about the Tapirapé Indians. Other surviving customs include gift giving and reciprocity, oratorical duels, manioc processing, belief in spirits, revenge killing, shamanism and body painting. Even his annoyed observation that women "would be after us incessantly, pestering us" for beads and other presents rings true. It can also be found in the work of Napoleon Chagnon and other contemporary anthropologists.

Montaigne's Morals

Léry's work served European writers and moralists well. Michel Montaigne, the sixteenth-century inventor of the essay as a literary form, wrote "On Cannibals" a few years after Léry's *History* appeared. Although he does not mention his sources, his account of the Tupi-speaking Indians of Brazil owes much to Léry:

> They spend the whole day dancing. Their young men go hunting after wild beasts with bows and arrows. Some of their women employ themselves in the meantime with the warming of their drink, which is their principal duty. In the morning, before they begin to eat, one of their old men preaches to the whole barnful, walking from one end to the other, and repeating the same phrase many times, until he has completed the round – for the buildings are quite a hundred yards long. He enjoins only two things upon them: valour against the enemy and love for their wives. (Montaigne 1984: 111)

Like Léry, Montaigne tries to draw moral lessons from Indian cannibalism, to the disadvantage and discomfiture of Europeans:

I am not so anxious that we should note the horrible savagery of these acts as concerned that, whilst judging their faults so correctly, we should be so blind to our own. I consider it more barbarous to eat a man alive than to eat him dead; to tear by rack and torture a body still full of feeling, to roast it by degrees, and then give it to be trampled and eaten by dogs and swine – a practice which we have not only read about but seen within recent memory, not between ancient enemies, but between neighbors and fellow-citizens and, what is worse, under the cloak of piety and religion – than to roast and eat a man after he is dead ... We are justified therefore in calling these people barbarians by reference to the laws of reason, but not in comparison with ourselves, who surpass them in every kind of barbarity. (1984: 113)

Montaigne had the rare experience of meeting three Tupi warriors who had been taken to France to be shown to the King. He reports asking them their opinions of the place. One replied that he could not understand how some people there could be so rich and some so poor. "They found it strange that ... they did not take the others by the throat or set fire to their houses" (1984: 119). That was still to come.

Rousseau and the Noble Savage

One of the theoreticians whose work would be used to justify the cataclysm of revolution was the eighteenth-century philosopher Jean-Jacques Rousseau. Like Montaigne, he probably read Léry and the other chroniclers and used them as sources for his essays. In *Émile*, his criticism of French mothering and condemnation of swaddling echo Léry, as does his characterisation of "savage man" in *A Discourse on the Origin of Inequality*. Like many social critics before and since, Rousseau used the savage as a foil to decadent European society.

Rousseau believed that humans were better off before the advent of metallurgy and agriculture. Private property resulted in rivalry and competition that he thought had not existed earlier. "The newborn state of society thus gave rise to a horrible state of war." Once inequality was established as the basis of social life, rules, laws and rulers emerged to lessen and govern conflict. While "the savage ... breathes only peace and liberty" and "desires only to live and be free from labour," civilised man "goes on in drudgery to his last moment, and even seeks death to put himself in a position to live, or renounces life to acquire immortality" (Rousseau 1950: 270).

This characterisation of the savage bears little resemblance to Léry's Tupinambá, who lived to kill and eat their enemies. But Rousseau echoes Léry and Montaigne in his contempt for civilisation: "That men are actually wicked, a sad and continual experience of them proves beyond doubt." It is only in "the state of nature" that "man is naturally good" (1950: 273).

Conquest and Contact

It took the development of technology and European domination to lead western social thinkers to conclude that the condition of humankind was improving and would continue to do so. Indigenous people could then be seen as noble only as long as they did not obstruct "the march of progress."

By the eighteenth century, much of the world was open to European penetration, exploitation and colonisation. In Brazil, bands of adventurers called *bandeirantes* (standard-bearers) started plunging into the interior in the seventeenth century, hunting slaves and prospecting for precious metals. They defied the Jesuits, who tried to protect indigenous groups by settling them in villages and teaching them "the arts of civilisation." For their efforts, the Jesuits were expelled from Brazil in 1759. By that time, however, plantation owners were increasingly using African slaves, and indigenous groups were fleeing deep into the Amazonian wilderness. Many of the peoples who had inhabited coastal areas were wiped out in conflicts with Europeans or by diseases brought by them. The estimated number of indigenous people in Brazil in 1500 varies from 2 million to 8 million; 400 years later, there were perhaps 150,000, most in remote areas. At the end of the twentieth century their population had doubled, to about 300,000, at least half of whom were under the age of 18.

Throughout the eighteenth century groups like the Kayapó were in retreat from the triumphant European invaders. Though hidden deep in the mountains, the Yanomami may have been in indirect contact with Europeans in the eighteenth century, via trade networks through which metal tools traveled. In addition, neighboring indigenous groups raided their area for slaves, whom they sold to whites. Portuguese slaving expeditions "reached a peak between about 1737 and 1755" (Ferguson 1995: 79–80); between 1740 and 1750, 20,000 slaves may have been taken from the upper Orinoco region. Although indigenous slavery was legally abolished in 1755, slavers operated in the Amazon throughout the nineteenth century. The way of life of the Yanomami and other indigenous groups has been threatened and affected by outsiders for quite a long time.

In the early nineteenth century, sentiment built for Brazil to declare its independence from Portugal. Even as the Brazilians began redefining themselves as a nation, they continued to import European fashions in clothing, literature and music. Soon after declaring independence in 1822, elite Brazilians rediscovered their native heritage and glorified their indigenous ancestors. Some changed their names or gave their children indigenous names. The products of this fashion included three romantic novels by José de Alencar (1829–77), *O Guarani, Ubirajara* and *Iracema*. Brazilian composer Carlos Gomes made *O Guarani* into an opera that achieved international success.

Alencar's Ancestors

Iracema is a simple tale, set in the sixteenth century, about a virtuous Indian princess who falls for a Portuguese invader allied with a rival tribe. In his preface, Alencar claims to tell a true story based on oral tradition, and cites Léry and other chroniclers as the sources of ethnographic details.

An archetypal figure, Iracema (the name is an anagram of "America") is doomed to die after she gives birth to the first mixed-race child in the province of Ceará, Alencar's home. She and the other Indian characters speak stilted prose, generally referring to themselves in the third person. Iracema leans against her lover's breast like a timid bird, tears are always trembling on her eyelids, she is perfectly submissive, and she waits alone in her "love nest" for her lover to return from his glorious deeds. Abandoned without explanation, she dies of a broken heart when her lover finally returns. He buries her under a palm tree, and her mixed-race son survives. At the end of the book, the lover's indigenous friend and battle companion is baptised. This is the happy ending Alencar's readers expected.

Iracema is the easily disposable progenitor of a mestizo culture, an allegorical figure rather than a fully formed character. The realities of indigenous peoples' brutal and tragic encounters with Europeans are nowhere to be found in this novel. As the Indians retreated far away, into Brazil's most remote areas, it became easier to romanticise them at a distance. On the frontiers, however, direct interactions between Brazilians and Indians were violent, often marked by mutual incomprehension, hatred or uneasy ambiguity. This mixed pattern of idealisation and contempt has continued until today.

Penetration

Visitors of all kinds have gone to the Amazon for the past 200 years. A tradition of scientific reporting, pioneered by Louis Agassiz and others, grew in tandem with travel literature that reflected the prejudices and insights of cosmopolitan outsiders, from Victorian explorer Sir Richard Burton to twentieth-century German novelist and critic Stefan Zwieg. Professional explorers braved the perils of the "Green Hell"; some, like Colonel Fawcett in the 1920s, were killed by Indians. President Theodore Roosevelt almost died on an Amazon expedition in 1914. A river previously unknown to outsiders bears his name.

Indians continued violently to resist incursions by would-be settlers, prospectors and other intruders until recent times. Kaingang Indians attacked workers installing telegraph lines in the populous southern state of Rio Grande do Sul in the 1920s. The Kayapó are still feared in their region because of their former practice of raiding their indigenous and non-indigenous neighbors. In response, the Brazilian government developed an ingenious way of making contact with indigenous groups and persuading them to stop attacking outsiders.

Under the leadership of General Cândido Rondon, who claimed indigenous ancestry, the Indian Protection Service (SPI) was founded in 1910. Rondon's credo was "Die if necessary but never kill." His agents set out to contact groups by following them into the bush and leaving them presents until they emerged for a non-violent encounter. Sometimes this process took months or even years. Unfortunately, the SPI became corrupt over the years and abandoned Rondon's model; after a series of scandals it was abolished in 1965 and replaced by the National Indigenous Foundation (FUNAI).

The Brothers Villas Boas

Among Rondon's inheritors were three brothers, Orlando, Claudio and Leonardo Villas Boas, who began their careers as protectors of Indians on a 1945 government expedition, which opened an unexplored area in Mato Grosso. Orlando and Claudio published *March to the West: The Epic of the Roncador-Xingu Expedition* in 1994, when they were in their 80s (Leonardo died young). They write vividly about the Indians of the Gê language group, who include the Kayapó and some of their neighbors. The Txucarramães (a Kayapó sub-group):

> ... constitute a powerful nation that has energetically resisted contact with whites. Deep-seated enemies of all the tribes, both neighboring and non-neighboring, [they] keep their territory shut off from any outsider through a permanent state of war. They keep constant vigilance over their habitats and trekking areas. For more than 50 years, they have been subjected to brutal pressure from the invading civilisation. There is no one who has not heard of the Kayapó, a nation feared for its haughtiness and rebelliousness, and currently one of the most numerous in our vast territory. (Villas Boas 1994: 560)[3]

It took months for the Villas Boas brothers to "attract" the Txucarramães by leaving gifts at the Indians' camps. They "suddenly appeared in front of the Juruna village ... Yelling and calling insistently, gesturing and shaking their bows, the 'wooden lips' neither showed nor inspired trust." (1994: 561).[4] On another occasion, a couple of years later, a group of Txucarramães appeared:

> ... painted with genipapo. They were very agitated, confused, making sweeping gestures and talking ceaselessly ... There were more than 50, mostly young men. Gathered in the hut, restless, nervous, some quite startled, they hid quickly in the bush, scarcely grabbing the presents we had left. (1994: 562)

At a second meeting, Kremuro, one of the Kayapó leaders, agreed to travel ten days upriver to the Brazilians' camp. On this excursion, the Villas Boas brothers discovered that the Txucarramães called themselves "Metotire" and "Mencragnotire." The latter are the people of Raoni, a young man at the time, who toured the world 30 years later with Sting.

After this journey and the Indians' return home, the Villas Boas brothers decided to meet the entire group. They took reporters along with them. Kremuro greeted them cordially but said he could not predict what would happen next. More and more Indians – finally about 400 – arrived. "Painted black, extremely agitated, they beat their breasts as they talked and didn't stay for a moment in the same place. It was as if they were walking on a hot griddle" (1994: 564).

A couple of days later, the Indians called for the Brazilians in the middle of the night. "On sleepily going down to the embarcation point, we were surrounded by more than 100 men painted black (a sign that they are angry), agitated, not one showing the comraderie of a few hours before" (1994: 566). The Indians told them that the women were afraid and insisted they go and reassure them. Leaving the journalists in camp, they went into the forest with the Kayapó, who grabbed each one by the wrist as they walked.

When they arrived at the Indian camp, no women were to be seen. "After being freed and placed in the middle of a circle of more than 200 men, painted black and carrying heavy clubs, we were told to call the women." The fire went out, and the Villas-Boas brothers shouted for it to be rekindled. An Indian yelled, "Kill the whites, they're no good." Suddenly an old woman came out of the forest and called for the other women. "The tension broke. Now the men were laughing. They laughed nervously, but they laughed" (1994: 568).

According to journalist Washington Novaes, the Villas Boas brothers had erred by offering the Kayapó:

> ... only presents that interested men: machetes, fishhooks, etc. Indignant, all the women of the village left. The men tried to attract them by preparing food and calling them – they stomped on the food and went away again. Furious, the men blamed Orlando, Claudio and their companions, who escaped only because an old woman took pity on them. (Grupioni 1994: 183)

Years later, the Villas Boas considered the Kayapó "attracted. They've left the state of war and are great friends of ours today."[5] In this story can be seen the Kayapó's mastery of the art of intimidation, which has served them well in their dealings with outsiders.

Orlando and Claudio concluded their account of the Kayapó with a poignant story of the return of a Brazilian captive who had lived with the Indians for 15 years. Krumare, a Kayapó leader, accompanied the young man to his home. On leaving, "Krumare hid his tears. In the boat, as soon as he sat down, he covered his face with his hands." Villagers waved goodbye as the boat pulled away, but "Krumare, in the same posture, did not want to look or respond. We tried to divert him. Nothing worked" (Villas Boas 1994: 576).

A few years later, the Villas Boas brothers founded the Xingu Indigenous Park, a large reserve where 17 indigenous groups still live peacefully and prosperously. Their health is the best of any indigenous groups in Brazil, and the Park is administered by an indigenous director.

Strangely, the brothers devote only two pages of their memoir to their heroic efforts to establish the park. They portray themselves primarily as nationalists, and only incidentally as protectors of indigenous peoples. In view of the massive impingements that now threaten so many Amazonian indigenous groups, the Villas Boas' description of the Roncador-Xingu Expedition's results sounds off-key: "Innumerable ranches began to be established in the region. With the villages that became cities, navigation was stimulated. Consolidating the progress, airlines were founded in various places" (1994: 611).

The Villas Boas brothers were *sertanistas*, professional backwoodsmen, not scholarly researchers. Brazilian and foreign anthropologists seem to have begun doing systematic field research on indigenous groups in the 1930s. Thus Claude Lévi-Strauss traveled from Paris to São Paulo and thence to central Brazil in the late 1930s, teaching at the new University of São Paulo and going on extended expeditions to collect indigenous artefacts and customs. He spent five years in Brazil and then went into exile in the USA during the Second World War. In 1955, back in Paris, he wrote *Tristes Tropiques*, apparently for a general audience with some knowledge of European literature and philosophy.

The Anthropologist as Existentialist

Widely read, *Tristes Tropiques* (Sad Tropics) influenced many Europeans' and North Americans' understanding of indigenous people. A richly allusive, highly literary mix of memoir, travelogue and monograph, it contains unforgettably eloquent passages, amusing anecdotes and profound meditations on nature and culture.

At the same time, it must have made its readers feel that Brazil's Indians were pathetic remnants of once-vital cultures, doomed to disappear or already gone. In contrast to Léry's Tupinambá:

> The societies we could study today, in conditions which it would be a great illusion to compare to those of four centuries ago, were enfeebled in body and mutilated in form ... This development had come as a monstrous and unintelligible cataclysm. (Lévi-Strauss 1967: 319)

In a melancholy meditation on the anthropologist's role, he says, "The investigator eats his heart out in the exercise of his profession ... The only apparent result is that his presence is forgiven by a handful of wretched people who will soon, in any case, be extinct" (1967: 374). It should be noted, however, that most of the groups he visited are still struggling to follow their traditional customs where he left them 60 years ago. They may not prosper, but they have survived.

Lévi-Strauss did not conduct ethnographic research according to the modern model, in which the anthropologist spends an extended period (usually at least a year) with one group, learning their language and sharing their life as a "participant-observer." Instead, he aimed "rather to understand the American continent as a whole than to deepen my knowledge of human nature by studying one particular case." He mounted large expeditions that entered areas previously unknown to Europeans. The first anthropologist to travel overland from Cuiabá to the Madeira River, he made the three-month trip with three other researchers, 15 backwoodsmen, 15 mules and 30 oxen pulling carts loaded with supplies. He would spend a few weeks with each indigenous group they encountered, doing a census, compiling a glossary of the group's language, drawing up genealogies, making an inventory of the group's material culture and observing daily life. This style of research gave him little opportunity to know the Indians as people. "If this was 'escape,'" he commented drily, "I was one of escape's bureaucrats."

Lévi-Strauss tended to objectify the Indians. The "indigence of the Nambikwara material culture" discouraged him as a collector of objects. He compares them to ants as they trek across the barren landscape and describes the young girls as "naked (and supple) as worms" (1967: 278). He seems more comfortable describing kinship systems and marriage rules or the beauties of nature than the people.

Lévi-Strauss' most famous work, which has come to be known as structural anthropology, is highly abstract and theoretical. For him, indigenous people are objects of study, "a pretext for aesthetic contemplation and disinterested meditation" (1967: 383). In *Tristes Tropiques*, he uses them as a vehicle for a pessimistic evaluation of the anthropological enterprise and the human condition. At the beginning he complains that he pursued experience "to the ends of the earth without managing either to decipher its meaning or to remain on intimate terms with it" (1967: 46).

In the concluding chapter, he repeats this note of regret and loss. "Did my decision [to stay in Brazil for five years] bespeak a profound incapacity to live on good terms with my own social group? Was I destined, in fact, to live in ever greater isolation from my fellows?" (1967: 375). This is (perhaps unintentionally) ironic, considering his inability, as a Jew, to return to France during the war. More broadly, he pessimistically declares the impossibility of doing anything to change society:

> The man who takes action in his own country cannot hope to understand the world outside; the man who takes all knowledge for his ambition must give up the idea of ever changing anything at home ... his place lies with "the others," and his role is to understand them. Never can he act in their name ... such a position could not but then prejudice his judgement. (1967: 384)

Other anthropologists have had a more energetic sense of their responsibility and capacity to act on behalf of the vulnerable people they study. While he reduces anthropologists to "mere spectators," Lévi-Strauss also says anthropology's ultimate goal is to reform our own society. How this change is to be undertaken, he does not say, however. His main concern is "to construct a theoretical model of a society which corresponds to none that can be observed in reality, but will help us to disentangle 'what in the present nature of Man is original, and what is artificial'" (1967: 391). (Here he quotes his philosophical ancestor, Rousseau.)

He concludes stoically: "It will eventually become plain that no human society is fundamentally good; but neither is any of them fundamentally bad." Human beings are, however, inherently destructive. "Man has never – save only when he reproduces himself – done other than cheerfully dismantle millions upon millions of structures to reduce their elements to a state in which they can no longer be reintegrated" (1967: 397).

And yet, writing in the 1950s (when existentialism reigned in France), Lévi-Strauss managed to offer one slim thread to lead us out of "the abyss we are so insanely creating." It is the choice between "appearance and nothing." In choosing, "I take on myself, unreservedly, my condition as a man" (1967: 398).

But he dances away from grand philosophical conclusions in the final paragraphs of *Tristes Tropiques*, as he wistfully calls for unmediated experience, "beyond thought and beneath society." This seems a long way from an account of the kinship system of the Nambikwara, who lived so simply that they slept on the ground and possessed no pots for him to take back to Paris. What then is this book about? Is its message as evanescent as the sunset he brilliantly describes in an early chapter? Why bother to learn about Indians, after all, if they are doomed to extinction and we to passivity?

Looking for the other, carrying a one-way mirror, we go with Lévi-Strauss to "the ends of the earth." Shadowy figures, the Indians are too far away, or too close, to see clearly. Hovering behind the glass, we finally focus only on ourselves.

Since the 1950s, increasing numbers of anthropologists from many countries have gone to Brazil's interior to study indigenous groups. The principal experts on the Yanomami and the Kayapó have been returning to the same groups for more than 25 years, acquiring unequalled knowledge and personal understanding of the people. Despite living in a less accessible region, the Yanomami have hosted more anthropologists and received more attention than the Kayapó. Perhaps this is because the Yanomami have become known as the "largest relatively uncontacted indigenous group in the Western Hemisphere." As scores of indigenous groups have disappeared from the map,[6] anthropologists have felt increasing urgency to study the groups most vulnerable to disease and invasion, while they still preserve the basic elements of their traditional cultures.

How Fierce?

Anthropologists studying the Kayapó disagree about how to interpret their culture, but the Yanomami have aroused far more controversy, both inside and outside the profession. For two decades, one US anthropologist, Napoleon Chagnon, had a virtual monopoly on the interpretation of Yanomami culture, though a few others had also been studying them for years. He published his famous ethnography, *Yanomamö, The Fierce People,* in 1968; since then, he estimates, 3–4 million US college students have read it in anthropology courses (Alcântara 1995: 8). For a long time his interpretation was accepted as authoritative by many, inside and outside academia. In the early 1980s he fought fiercely with anthropologists who disagreed with him, but these disputes had no impact outside the discipline. Then highly publicised battles over Yanomami culture blew up in the late 1980s, during the massive gold rush that decimated the group.

In 1988 Chagnon published an article in *Science* that purported to explain the Yanomami's propensity for violence as the effect of "reproductive effort." Yanomami men who killed more people had greater access to women and produced more children, he claimed. At a time when sociobiology was going out of fashion in the academic world, Chagnon insisted on basing his analysis on it. More important, Brazilian government officials and politicians who supported the gold rush tried to use the article to justify the end of the Yanomami. Soon after its publication in *Science*, a Portuguese translation appeared in one of Brazil's most important newspapers, and Brazilian politicians were still paraphrasing it in interviews and speeches six years later.

Brazilian and French anthropologists who had studied the Yanomami for extended periods tried to protect them from genocide by leading a charge against Chagnon. They published letters challenging his data and analysis in the *Anthropology Newsletter*, one of the official publications of the American Anthropological Association. Chagnon reacted with rage worthy of a Yanomami warrior. Or maybe not – anthropologist Jacques Lizot, who lived with the Yanomami for 20 years, said, "The [fierce] man is calm; he remains silent, but when he does get up from his hammock, it is in order to strike the one who is bothering him, and to strike without uttering a single word" (Lizot 1994: 857). The fight between Chagnon and his critics has simmered in anthropological periodicals ever since.

Chagnon seems perpetually unaccustomed to being challenged or contradicted. He lashes out, using liberal amounts of sarcasm and hyperbole and accusing his enemies of being motivated by jealousy or ambition. He seems to have no respect for anybody's theory but his own. Experts who have spent more time with the Yanomami than he has are scorned as not knowing what they are talking about. If they charge him with subscribing to a discredited and outmoded form of social Darwinism, he replies that they hate Darwinism or are unscientific. If they challenge the accuracy of his data, he calls them pseudo-scientific. Even scholars who are careful not to criticise him personally arouse his wrath, merely for raising questions about his general approach. And if all else fails, he threatens to sue.

The pyrotechnics exploding around Chagnon have made it difficult to calmly evaluate the validity of his work. Suffice it to say that his image of the fierce Yanomami still dominates the minds of anthropologists and non-anthropologists, and much of the debate over the Yanomami responds to or reacts against it.

The fourth edition of his ethnography, retitled *Yanomamö, the Last Days of Eden*, was published in 1992, the year of the Earth Summit. Without acknowledging that he is responding to critics, Chagnon qualifies or backs away from earlier conclusions and shows some changes in attitude. He is now careful to say, "The Yanomami with whom I work" or "the area I work in," instead of generalising about all the Yanomami (who are divided into four or five linguistic sub-groups, spread across a vast area in two countries, and in varying degrees of contact with outsiders). Nevertheless, in the passages from earlier editions, he often slips into generalisations about the entire culture or uses the present tense to describe customs that may have disappeared as a result of contact.

Although he says the Yanomami fight mostly over women, he cites plenty of cases in which they fight about witchcraft directed at children or food theft. Ritualistic combats at inter-village feasts often become pitched battles that may have nothing to do with women. He avoids discussing infanticide and taboos against sexual activity that may limit the population. In general, he has little to say about women and their roles.

After the uproar over the *Science* article and the genocide of 1987–91, as well as political conflicts in which he was involved in Venezuela, Chagnon apparently felt he had to deal with the effects of the outside world on the Indians. He decided to become an applied anthropologist, since those already acting on behalf of the Yanomami "are doing it all wrong" (Chagnon 1992: 244). He excused himself for not speaking out in defense of the Yanomami during the gold rush by saying, "It took me some time [after a 1985 visit] to marshal the data necessary to demonstrate the problems" (Chagnon 1992: 287). Yet other anthropologists were denouncing the genocide at the same time he published the *Science* article. In 1992 he was finally ready to acknowledge, "It is patently obvious, however, that there is much suffering and sickness among the [genocide] survivors, particularly malaria and respiratory infections" brought in by miners (Chagnon 1992: 291).

As part of his conversion to applied anthropology, Chagnon announced he had founded the Yanomamö Survival Fund and was involved in another organisation called American Friends of Venezuelan Indians. "Now I want to make sure that [the Yanomami] and their children get a fair shake in the inevitable changes that are occurring ... I cannot do that except by becoming an advocate of their right to a decent future ... The rest of my useful career will be devoted to them" (Chagnon 1992: 292).

Chagnon then makes an eloquent plea for citizen action:

What you and I do now might make a big difference ... If the Yanomami go down, so also might many other native peoples, along with the biospheres they have been keeping intact. The Yanomami are a symbol for all tribal peoples and their habitats everywhere – perhaps the ultimate test case of whether ordinary concerned people can stay a destructive process whose course is inexorable if you and I do nothing about it. (Chagnon 1992: 294)

Chagnon has repeatedly criticised other anthropologists, missionaries and non-governmental organisations for "competing among themselves to see if they can get the title of sole representative of the Indians in the outside world" and has charged them with transforming the Yanomami into a commodity. "Whoever manages to establish himself as the exclusive owner of the Yanomami cause will be in the money," he told a Brazilian news magazine in 1995 (Alcântara 1995: 8). This is a common canard in Brazil. But nobody acquainted with the anthropologists, missionaries and NGOs who actually defend the Yanomami has seen them getting rich in the process; quite the contrary. Chagnon has become far more prosperous from his book royalties. It seems just that he invest some of his profits in the people to whom he owes his success.

The American Friends of Venezuelan Indians went out of existence in 1997. According to its lawyer, it "never got off the ground because of political turmoil in Venezuela." A 1997 letter to the Yanomamö Survival Fund was "Returned to Sender, Not Deliverable."[7] It is not unusual for such non-profit organisations to fail. They often do not manage to raise sufficient funds to operate, or their projects are unviable, or they cannot obtain the cooperation of people on the ground. Without these vehicles to help the Yanomami, how will Chagnon fulfill his pledge to devote himself to their welfare?

The Yanomami require considerable assistance, especially in the areas of health and education, to ensure their future survival as a people. With the halting cooperation of the Brazilian government and modest international funding, a consortium of non-profit and religious organisations is trying to provide health care and schooling to them. They need all the help they can get.

Other Versions of the Yanomami

Meanwhile, the long intellectual dispute over Yanomami violence continues. In 1995, Brian Ferguson, who specialises in the anthropology of war but has no Yanomami field experience, published *Yanomami Warfare*. After surveying the extant literature on the Yanomami, he proposed a theory to explain the ebb and flow of violence over hundreds of years and across their vast territory.

European slavers invaded southern Venezuela and northern Brazil in the seventeenth and eighteenth centuries. With them came western goods, especially metal tools that the indigenous groups of the region prized. Although most of the slavers withdrew in the early nineteenth century (and the Yanomami may have retreated deeper into the mountains), the tools continued to circulate throughout the Yanomami's extensive trading network. In the late nineteenth century, a renewed supply of trade goods entered the area during a shortlived rubber boom.

Ferguson relates waves of direct and indirect contact in the twentieth century to increases and decreases in the level of violence among the Yanomami. Contact led to epidemics and higher death rates. The Yanomami believed these deaths were caused by witchcraft by enemy villages. Conflicts ensued within and between villages. When outsiders withdrew (as they did periodically, sometimes for long periods), the scarcity of trade goods could also cause conflicts.

Ferguson believes increasing polygamy among the Yanomami is a recent phenomenon. For him, the acquisition of women is a side-effect, not a cause, of violence. The principal cause is competition for coveted trade goods.

According to the literature Ferguson surveyed, the Yanomami have never been "truly isolated." Their situation has always been affected by events outside. When they found out that neighboring indigenous groups had obtained trade goods, the Yanomami raided them or even abased themselves to them, begging or working in exchange for tools. Such relationships could continue for years. Ferguson paints a very different picture of the Yanomami from Chagnon, who calls them "sovereign and in complete control of their own destiny until only a few years ago" (Chagnon 1992: 1).

When more goods enter the Yanomami universe, Ferguson says, war decreases or stops. But then come genocide and epidemics, which are far more devastating. Some Yanomami have settled at missions, which give some protection from predatory outsiders. But when the Indians become sedentary, the game supply in the area decreases as a result of over-hunting, and so do food sharing and solidarity. Theft becomes a problem; interpersonal violence increases. In recent years this situation, which

Chagnon and others have documented, has resulted from invasions by gold miners on both sides of the border.

Yanomami warfare, Ferguson concludes, "is the result of a major change in access to western manufactures" (1995: 195).

But even according to Chagnon's statistics, three-quarters of Yanomami deaths are due to disease, not internal violence. The greatest threat to their survival comes from outside, not from their belligerence to one another.

Ferguson also questions Chagnon's contention that most Yanomami conflicts are over women. In the long term, he says, only a minority of recorded fights concerned women. Most were related to "demographic disruption" caused by deaths due to disease. Men with more trade goods (not, as Chagnon contends, men with more killings) had greater access to women.

Unlike Chagnon, Ferguson explains Yanomami violence as a historical, not a biological, phenomenon. Their patterns of warfare have nothing to do with "our evolutionary past," he insists, but with the events of the past 300 years or so.[8]

All kinds of outsiders have affected the Yanomami. For example, Ferguson says, Napoleon Chagnon's behavior in the field was "highly disruptive to the Yanomami" in the 1960s. Like other visitors, Chagnon distributed metal tools as presents, and his method of distribution may have created competition within and between villages that led to conflict.[9] From the 1970s on, more serious disruptions occurred after some missionaries gave away or exchanged guns and ammunition for work. In addition to less deadly clubs, arrows or blows, the Yanomami now use firearms in their internecine conflicts.

Ferguson states flatly, "At present, there simply are no data that substantiate the claim that aggressive behavior is associated with reproductive success among the Yanomami" (Ferguson 1995: 362). Nonetheless, he sees the Yanomami not as passive victims but as "aggressively pursuing their own interests." They have "shaped a political milieu in response to the intrusive white presence, which itself is largely beyond their control" (1995: 367).

For Ferguson, who has studied war for more than a decade, it "is not a natural state of affairs for human societies ... not the normal condition, leaving peace the state that needs to be explained ... War is not self-perpetuating. The costs are too high. But war can be self-reinforcing" (1995: 370). Although Chagnon and his rival, Jacques Lizot, seem to agree that warfare is endemic among all primitive peoples, Ferguson says this idea is "empirically unsupportable."

There are many problems with Ferguson's argument.[10] In focusing on inter-village warfare, he largely neglects interpersonal violence such as wife-beating. The Yanomami seem ready to fight over almost anything; both scarcity and plenty seem to trigger violence. In some areas but not others, depending on who is doing the reporting and when, violence is endemic or almost non-existent. Neither the literature he quotes nor Ferguson himself is consistent. An adequate assessment of his work requires a reviewer who is both an expert on the Yanomami and an evenhanded judge.

Ferguson's great accomplishment is his scrupulous examination of all the available source material and his careful attempt to build an explanatory framework. Even Chagnon praises his "noteworthy command of the anthropological literature ... He certainly has done his homework and is to be congratulated for the thoroughness of his efforts at researching the published sources in several languages" (Chagnon 1996: 671). He has not managed to construct the definitive explanation, however. The argument over the reasons for Yanomami violence will continue as long as we insist on seeing "something of all of us in the Yanomami, and something of them in all of us" (Chagnon 1992: xvii).

Ever since Europeans first encountered indigenous people on the beaches of America, both the invaders and the conquered have been trying to figure out who and what the other is. In the outsiders' squinting eyes, the Indians have been enemies of Christ, souls to save, subhuman brutes, unsatisfactory slaves, noble savages, passive victims, proud and virtuous warriors, vestiges of the stone age, saviours of the environment or unfit to survive. At least some of the Indians saw Europeans as "subhumans, peripheral and unintelligible" (Albert 1995: 5).

The great challenge for anthropologists has been to try to see others as they see themselves and then to portray them as people. This is a tremendously difficult undertaking. All of our common history stands between us and gets in the way of understanding. Our overblown sense of ourselves also blocks our view. Even the best-intended attempts at understanding may be misused by somebody else. From time to time, however, observers break through their self-created obstacles and show the shape of the other without too much distortion. This may happen only sporadically, unpredictably, in a few paragraphs scattered in a 400-page volume.

In the works of Léry, Montaigne, Lévi-Strauss, Ferguson and others, that shock of recognition keeps coming: no, the other is not myself, but someone else for whom I, too, am the other. We are, after all, members of the same paradoxical species; but despite our brilliance, we still do not fully comprehend one another. The effort to understand continues, while children die, forests fall and mercury pollutes the waters.

3

The People from Between the Waters[1]

In the early colonial history of Brazil, the Kayapó were known by the Portuguese as "the most treacherous of all the heathen" (Hemming 1978: 405). Numbering in the thousands, they occupied a large area between the Tocantins and Araguaia Rivers. They planted sweet potatoes, manioc, corn, bananas and tobacco and spent several months of the year trekking, hunting and gathering in forests and savannahs, and raiding their indigenous neighbors.

When the Kayapó encountered white prospectors, slavers and other intruders in their territories, they gave no quarter, since "none was given to them" (Hemming 1978: 405). As late as the

Kayapó leaders visit Tucurui Dam, 1988.
Photo by Vincent Carelli, Centro de Trabalho Indigenista.

1950s, they were known as "the terror of the civilised" (Verswijver 1978). The Portuguese used other indigenous groups, the Kayapó's traditional enemies, to mount punitive expeditions against them over the centuries. Another, much larger, Gê-language group, the Southern Kayapó, was apparently wiped out in these conflicts, but the Northern Kayapó, the ancestors of today's Kayapó communities, survived.

How the Kapayó Lived

According to Dennis Werner, an anthropologist who studied the Kayapó's subsistence pattern during the 1970s, their traditional way of life was "a stable one, which took advantage of the resources of a varied habitat. Although population density was low, this mixed strategy probably supported a larger population more reliably than would have been possible either by hunting and gathering alone or by greater dependence on agriculture" (Werner *et al.* 1982: 214).

By the early nineteenth century, the Kayapó were retreating west of the Araguaia River. During the nineteenth century they came into contact with settlers and missionaries, not always with violent results. Their first recorded peaceful contact with whites occurred in 1859, when a group of Kayapó visited a missionary post, where they remained until 1882. Until the present, they have had an ambivalent relationship with the outsiders who have encountered them.

At the end of the nineteenth century, most of the Northern Kayapó (about 4,000 people) lived in two large villages in the Xingu region and roamed among campsites in a 200-kilometer radius. They were renowned for their ferocity, not only to whites but to one another and other indigenous groups. Kayapó villages often split, as a result of conflicts between men's age-sets or moieties (men's houses) that divided communities in two. According to anthropologist Terence Turner, who has studied the Kayapó since the early 1960s, these conflicts expressed "the fundamental tension at the heart of traditional Kayapó social organisation, which the structure of Kayapó institutions simultaneously generated and sought ... to contain" (Turner 1991a: 17).

During the course of the nineteenth century, Kayapó men began to obtain firearms, either by trading with or raiding settlers and other indigenous groups. They used these weapons in their internal disputes, as well as in conflicts with outsiders. Numbers of

Kayapó killed in internal fights were usually low, but since the villages that split off were small, the killings had a great impact.

From the two main villages existing at the end of the nineteenth century, at least 14 communities have formed as a result of these conflicts. A few small Kayapó groups are still "isolated," uncontacted by whites and rarely seen by other Kayapó.

Trading and Raiding

Throughout the twentieth century the Kayapó have had a mixed relationship with their non-indigenous neighbors, who included missionaries, rubber tappers and other extractivists, ranchers and squatters. On the one hand, Werner *et al.* (1979: 305) observed, they "participate in cash exchange on regional markets, selling forest products, artisanry, labor or other goods." On the other hand, until the 1950s they frequently raided white settlements to obtain firearms, ammunition, cloth, beads, hammocks, metal pots and other goods. These attacks were sometimes deadly.

Internal conflicts have continued – over women, ritual duties and other local issues. Over time the moiety system (which seems to have triggered splits) declined. The new villages had populations ranging from 25 to a few hundred, and only one men's house per community. As the Kayapó came into more regular contact with whites, they were often decimated by contagious diseases such as influenza and malaria. According to Turner (1991a: 42), one group lost 50 per cent of its population of 240 in a single year, 1958. In general, however, the Kayapó's fearsome reputation and behavior served them well. They and other warlike peoples "survived in greater numbers and in better health" than more pacific indigenous groups (Schmink and Wood 1992: 261).

In the mid-1930s the Kayapó first encountered Brazilian government agents from the SPI, the Indian protection agency, which later became renowned for its ineffectuality and corruption. The SPI moved Kayapó villages to get them away from Brazilian settlements, diseases and goods, and the Kayapó continued to fight amongst themselves and to move away from one another. The period from the 1930s to the 1970s must have been a tragic time for them, with villages wracked by conflict and disease. Unlike hundreds of other Brazilian indigenous groups in this century, however, the Kayapó were not wiped out by the disastrous effects of contact with Brazilian society.

Leading Men and Women

Part of the reason may be luck, but the decisive leadership of some Kayapó men and women has also been important in ensuring their survival as a culture. They took advantage of the presence or proximity of outsiders to attend school, learn Portuguese and gain some experience of non-indigenous people and culture. Later they used this knowledge to become politically influential inside Kayapó society (Turner 1992a: 319).

In the 1950s, Raoni (also called Rob-ni or Rop-ni) first appeared on the scene as an intermediary between the Villas Boas brothers and the Mekragnoti (who had split into three communities after breaking away from Gorotire around 1905). As we have seen in Chapter 2, the Villas Boas brothers played a vital role in protecting dozens of Central Brazilian indigenous groups from extinction, by founding the Xingu Indigenous Park and by acting as peacemakers among indigenous groups and between them and the Brazilians.

Raoni is not the only important chief among the Kayapó – each village usually has three to six influential men who dominate local politics – but he has acquired local, national and international prominence over the past 30 years. He became a leader not through kinship ties but because of his skills as an orator inside the village and as a diplomat to the Brazilians (Verswijver 1978: 56). Turner, who has known Raoni for many years, says he "is generally recognised as the dominant leader and personality of the community, and indeed has become a nationally famous spokesman for indigenous rights, a role duly recognised by his compatriots in Kapot [his home village]" (Turner 1991a: 37).

A Kayapó community became part of the newly founded Xingu Park in 1961, moving to an area near its northern border. Ten years later, when the population had reached more than 200, the Brazilian army and Interior Ministry "secretly rerouted the construction of one of the main roads of the new Trans-Amazonian highway system, BR-080, so as to cut off the northern 20 per cent of the area of the Xingu Park" – exactly the area where the Kayapó lived (Turner 1978: 18). The Villas Boas brothers, then administering the Park, wanted the Kayapó to move 40 kilometers south to escape what would surely be deadly contact with the highway construction crews and the settlers who would later use and live along the road. Raoni led a faction supporting this move, while a more militant group split off and went in the opposite direction.

A few Kayapó staged a daring raid on the roadhead, terrorising the crew, capturing a motor boat and sinking a tug. The "war" faction lost out, but years later young Kayapó warriors were using the captured boat to patrol their territory along the Xingu River. "The Kayapó have been quite effective in their role as a border patrol of the northern part of the Park, as at least a dozen trespassers have learned at the cost of their lives over the past 10 years (many others have been either turned away or expelled by less extreme but nonetheless forceful measures)" (Turner 1978: 19).

By 1984 the Brazilian government had returned the "stolen" area in the northern part of the Park to the Mekragnoti. In 1992, Tu'ire, Payakan's relative, told a conference at the University of Pennsylvania, "When whites come illegally into our territory, first we cut their arms with piranha teeth and kick them out. If they come back again, then we get really rough." Turner estimates that between 1970 and 1990, the Kayapó killed some 30 intruders, "and many others were driven off by armed attacks" (Turner 1978: 19).

In the late 1970s, the Kayapó were known throughout Brazil as formidable opponents. They used shortwave radio to warn one another of incursions, and warriors patrolled the territory, expelling intruders with calculated brutality. Nevertheless, invasions increased as the federal government kept delaying demarcation. In 1981, "16 Kayapó chiefs came together for an unprecedented ten-day meeting. Some of the participants in that historic gathering reportedly had not seen one another for nearly 40 years. The urgent need to protect their territory brought the Kayapó together ..." (Schmink and Wood 1992: 263).

The Front Lines of Contact

Attention focused on Gorotire, near where gold was discovered in the late 1970s. The village had become important in the 1950s, when Kayapó from elsewhere moved there to be near the missionary health post. But the Kayapó kept fighting amongst themselves, and immigrants to Gorotire were sometimes killed or driven away.

In the early 1980s Gorotire became the center of gold mining in the Kayapó Indigenous Area. After many conflicts with thousands of Brazilian prospectors, the Gorotire made a deal with the federal government, whereby they would allow the prospectors to mine gold in exchange for demarcation of their territory and a percentage of the mining proceeds. Payakan, who later toured the world defending Kayapó interests, played a key role in the conflicts and in the subsequent negotiations with the government.

The Gorotire monitored mining operations, doing complete body searches of all those leaving the area, to prevent smuggling. They also monitored all transactions between prospectors and gold buyers. By plane they regularly escorted the proceeds to the bank in Redenção. Paid employees in an office in the city attended to the needs of visiting Gorotire.

CEDI, a Brazilian NGO, reported in the late 1980s:

> During the dry season, they usually arrive in small or full-sized trucks from their fleet of 12 vehicles, driven by hired drivers. During the rainy season, they use their small plane and pay for innumerable air taxi rides. A large part of the funds pays for lodging and supermarket purchases. But there are also large outlays for employees' salaries, air shipping and gas for vehicles and for the village generator, which consumes 40,000 liters of diesel per month. (CEDI 1991: 311)

This kind of contact with Brazilian society strongly affected the Kayapó, both directly and indirectly, materially and psychologically. The Kayapó's notorious ferocity became a symbolic weapon, which they used to intimidate outsiders as well as one another. At the same time, they were becoming increasingly dependent on the outside world.

Kinds of Conflict

In recounting the history of the Kayapó people, Turner focused on internal conflict because it was prevalent among them for centuries. Their acquisition of firearms in the nineteenth century had dramatic effects: a high level of both internal and external conflict "militarised" Kayapó society and created an "arms race" among them, "with gun-less groups suffering devastating attacks by groups already possessing guns" (Turner 1991a: 48).

By the 1940s, "raiding for some groups had become a regular means of acquiring a wide variety of Brazilian commodities" (Turner 1991a: 48). The Kayapó had become dependent on their enemies, the whites, for goods that they wanted but had no way of producing themselves. Citing oral histories, Verswijver estimated that the Mekragnoti carried out 92 raids between 1905 and the 1950s (Turner 1992a: 329).

Outcry from settlers led the federal government to send pacification missions to contact the Kayapó. These expeditions carried yet more goods that the Kayapó wanted, from fishhooks to cooking pots. By the time the groups were "pacified" in the 1950s, Turner observed, "warfare with the Brazilians had come to mean dependency on Brazilian society for commodities, and peace was seen primarily as a continuation of war by other means" (Turner 1992a: 330). The Kayapó seem to have made a pragmatic, tactical decision to reduce raiding and confine outright warfare to the expulsion of people they defined as trespassers. In Turner's words, they had "learned to need" the whites' goods and wanted to obtain more as easily as possible, and so over time they substituted various kinds of trade arrangements for warfare.

From 1900 to the 1950s, charismatic war leaders intensified their power within Kayapó communities. The old balance between groups inside the society was broken, perhaps permanently. Leaders and their followers "could justify their activities and dramatise their importance as the suppliers of the essential means of communal survival" (Turner 1991a: 64). Their power base was independent of the traditional social structure. Men's houses became "mutually independent military organisations" separate from the community as a whole (Turner 1991a: 60).

Chiefs derived their power from their ability to withdraw with their followers and start or join another village. Raoni, Pombo and Payakan all demonstrated their leadership in this way. Traditionally carried out in association with rituals like the New Corn Ceremony, treks became "vehicles for the expression of tension and opposition between rival groups within a single community" (Turner 1991a: 62). They all too easily turned into raiding parties. Instead of being months-long expeditions, treks became short forays, losing some of their ritual content. Since the 1950s, treks have remained short. This change may have altered dietary patterns, making the Kayapó more dependent on outside food products that only money could buy.

In recent years relations with the outside world have become ever more important, and as such the focus of political activity. Likewise, "the ownership or control of commodities ... became, in itself, an increasingly important token and source of status within the community" (Turner 1991a: 73). The balance of Kayapó society was altered, with families and households acquiring more importance at the expense of age-sets and other extra-familial institutions. Kayapó society began to lose some of its distinctive, traditional characteristics.

Consumers of Culture

In recent years the Kayapó have compensated for these changes by turning back to ceremonies as a focus of community life and "as the institutional means of expressing the unity of the community in opposition to the encompassing alien society" (Turner 1991a: 74). Kayapó of all ages may be found in the villages watching videos that Kayapó film-makers have produced of recent ceremonies.

Their demands for high-technology consumer goods, and their willingness to sell their natural resources in order to obtain them, show that the Kayapó are as sophisticated and discerning as any member of the international bourgeoisie. Like the rest of the modern world, however, Kayapó society has its own "loyal opposition" of critics, moralists and environmentalists, who call into question the wisdom of modern production and consumption patterns. Raoni, Payakan and other community leaders have played this role over the years. Furthermore, the Kayapó and their leaders have had to cope with constant threats to their culture and survival – serious threats from outside that they can neither ignore nor palliate.

International Diplomacy

Charismatic leaders such as Raoni and Payakan have transformed venerable patterns of political action by mobilising their followers for rituals of protest that have provided an alternative to raiding, internal violence and communal schisms. Instead of trying to obtain much-desired goods through dependency relations with merchants, local authorities, missionaries or government bureaucrats, in recent years they have gone to the top of the national and international system in defense of their vital interests.

The Kayapó have chosen their allies carefully and worked hard to accomplish their goals. Raoni took on the herculean task of finding a backer for the demarcation of Mekragnoti territory in the 1980s, when the Brazilian government balked at carrying out its statutory responsibility. He set out to conquer Sting, on whom he made a powerful impression when they first met in 1987.

In a 1993 interview with film-maker Geoffrey O'Connor, Sting called Raoni "definitely a leader, he carries himself as a warrior. I took him to huge cities in western Europe – to Paris – he wasn't fazed at all, because he has great self-esteem and understanding of his place in the world." In his talk-show appearances with Sting, Raoni was charismatic, yet patient and good-humored. As Sting described it:

> I would sing a song – that was the price – and Raoni would get up and talk – deliver his message, which is a very compelling message. It triggered a groundswell of appreciation of the problem in the rainforest and also how that problem relates to everyone on the planet. It's not something that's somewhere else, it's very connected to everyone. That message has been very successful. (O'Connor 1993)

Although he was defending and advancing Kayapó interests as a diplomat representing a nation, Raoni shrewdly presented himself as an environmentalist to international audiences. In visiting Kayapó territory, however, Sting had the opportunity to see that the issue was more than environmental:

> It's very apparent as you travel towards the rainforest from Brasilia, you fly over what is virtually a red barren desert, which was formerly very lush virgin rainforest, and then you hit the wall of the jungle, which is extraordinarily beautiful, and so the contrast of what it was and what it is is quite a shock. And you meet the people there and you hear their story, and you realise that without their environment they are going to be sucked into the lowest part of Brazilian society, which is basically slavery. (O'Connor 1993)

Sting's 1988 world tour with Raoni was only the beginning of his involvement with the Kayapó. He had promised Raoni that he would ensure the demarcation of the Mekragnoti reserve. After visiting the President of Brazil in a futile quest for official commitment to demarcation (and weathering negative publicity for his efforts inside and outside Brazil), Sting realised he could not carry out his commitment alone. He founded the Rainforest Foundation (RFF) and a Brazilian offshoot, the Fundação Mata Virgem (FMV), with anthropologists and professional administrators. Then he returned to his musical career.

The Foundation's first priority was to demarcate Mekragnoti territory. Three years' collaboration between RFF and FMV resulted in the first privately funded demarcation of a Brazilian indigenous reserve, in 1992. Sting observed:

When the Brazilian government let us demarcate that land, which is the size of Switzerland, I realized that all of that pain and all of that stuff that went down was actually worth it, because it's quite a significant victory, which could possibly be repeated. I don't see why it shouldn't be repeated. We haven't saved that area, we've set up the infrastructure so it can be protected. But it's still a significant victory. (O'Connor 1993)

The Rainforest Foundation also supported grassroots development projects among the Kayapó and other indigenous groups in Brazil. Sting raised funds for the Foundation's operations by giving yearly benefit concerts at New York's Carnegie Hall; by 1997 he had raised about $8 million for RFF, some $600,000 of which paid for the Mekragnoti demarcation. In the mid-1990s RFF began to extend its project work to Guyana, the Philippines and Papua New Guinea.

Through direct involvement, Sting came to understand the complexities of "saving the rainforest."

At first it seemed very simple: let's stop chopping down the rainforest, let's support these people. But the complexity of the issue when you take in the whole of Brazil and the Indians' needs themselves – vis-à-vis the forest, it's much less simple than I originally thought ... It's been a learning process for me, and I've realised a miracle is not going to happen ... All we can really hope to do is slow the process down of the destruction of the forest, so that people come to their senses. (O'Connor 1993)

Having witnessed the Kayapó's struggle to survive economically, Sting came to an unexpected conclusion:

The real problem is, how do you stop the logging? I think it's better that if there is going to be logging, the Indians control it themselves, because they have a stake in sustainable development, they have a stake in not leaving it as scorched earth ... And so – this is quite a different thing – how do you sell the idea of the Indians logging themselves? And yet they are probably the only people who could do it in a responsible way. (O'Connor 1993)

With and without Sting, the Kayapó made a spectacular impression on the international public in the late 1980s and early 1990s.

But this external political involvement carries on a tradition that goes back at least a hundred years.

The Kayapó:

> ... have always had an acute recognition of the hierarchical nature of Brazilian society. This is based in part on their own conception of hierarchy as it obtains in their own social structure. Since the very beginning of the contacts with Brazilian society, this has allowed them to formulate very effective strategies aimed at getting the attention of higher ups. (Fisher 1994: 225)

Since the nineteenth century the Kayapó have maintained trade relations with white settlers, merchants and landowners. Government pacification efforts in the 1950s effectively ended raiding. Since then, the Kayapó have used other tactics, such as organised but symbolic forms of intimidation, against merchants and landowners to win concessions from the government.

Government's Ambiguous Role

Meanwhile, Brazil was changing. The military government's development model in the 1960s and 1970s was meant to replace traditional extractive economies in the Amazon region. Federal agencies came to towns like Altamira, along with construction firms, mining companies and logging firms. The new Indian protection agency, FUNAI, stepped in to try to become the Kayapó's intermediary in making deals with private enterprises.

But FUNAI and other federal agencies failed to fulfill their statutory responsibilities to the Indians, while the big companies offered them health care, air transport, goods and infrastructural improvements in exchange for access to land and resources on the reserves (Fisher 1994: 225). In 1984 the Azzayp logging firm agreed to build a saw mill, three guardhouses, 14 wood houses, a clinic, two airstrips, a 70-kilometer-long road and a fence around 50 *alqueires* (about 136 hectares) of land that were to be cleared for pasture, in exchange for rights to extract mahogany from the Kikretum village region (CEDI 1991: 315). It was Pombo, Raoni's rival, who brokered this lucrative deal, for which he no doubt won as much prestige among his "constituents" as any Chicago alderman.

Over time the focus of power and decision shifted from local economic actors to FUNAI, and the Kayapó began visiting the agency's regional offices. "By their belligerent presence and demands," Fisher noted (1994: 225), "the Kayapó created discomfort among administrators that often resulted in compliance with Kayapó requests." They had discerned that top-level FUNAI officials sometimes shifted resources from one indigenous group to another, "depending on the pressure applied rather than by identification of specific needs."

Their Hour Upon the Stage

Thus the Kayapó became important political actors on the state and federal levels. When the Constituent Assembly was drawing up Brazil's new Constitution in 1987–8, the Kayapó went *en masse* to Brasilia to lobby on behalf of indigenous interests. There they conducted "demonstrations, sit-ins, meetings with leaders in which they asserted themselves in a threatening manner" (Fisher 1994: 226). They attracted considerable media attention by wearing warpaint, elaborate feather head-dresses and beads, and carrying war clubs as they sat watching the proceedings from the Congressional visitors' gallery.

In 1988, Payakan and Kuben-I clashed with the Brazilian government over hydroelectric development plans and received international attention and support. Through their highly publicised actions in Belém and other rituals of protest, the Kayapó became the most visible and famous indigenous group in Brazil, and the most politically powerful.

The Grande Carajás Project and other mega-projects of the 1970s and 1980s marked the internationalisation of Amazon development, financed through foreign bank loans, multilateral lending institutions like the World Bank and transnational corporations. Indigenous people in the Amazon immediately felt the economic, political and environmental effects of these projects and accompanying large-scale investment in cattle ranching, plantation and export agriculture, and mining. Now the sources of benefits had moved beyond FUNAI to other, more powerful federal agencies, international banks and intergovernmental bodies. This change "affected the Kayapó's ability to defend themselves and maintain their place within the region" (Fisher 1994: 226). As they figured out ways to benefit from selling access to natural resources such as mahogany and gold, the Kayapó became important economic actors. Their formidable abilities to organise and mobilise for political action helped them capitalise on their new economic position to an extent that few other indigenous groups have managed.

The special connections between para-statal enterprises, multi-national capital and government agencies meant that Kayapó rituals of protest aimed at any one of these sectors would have an impact on the others, especially if they could gain media attention. This was as true on the international as on the national or regional level.

With planning decisions coming from Brasilia, the Kayapó no longer gained much by focusing their pressure on local officials or regionally based agencies. Characteristically, they adapted to the changed situation by going to the top of the power structure. Thus the Kayapó have continued traditional war making, raiding and trekking through their own distinctive brand of international diplomacy, traveling to the First World to gain allies at the highest levels, financial support and prestige goods to show the folks back home. (Raoni's favorite in the early 1990s was a baseball cap with a stuffed cloth fish mounted on top.) As economic, social and political conditions keep changing, the Kayapó will keep developing new strategies to defend their interests, their culture and their resources.

Entrepreneurs and Rentiers

The Kayapó's success as international symbols of environmentalism has been transient, however, especially in light of their propensity for making deals with loggers and miners. "For a Kayapó to be an environmentalist today is in some senses similar to being a warrior in other times" (Fisher 1991: 29). But defending the environment is not an end in itself for the Kayapó.

There is a danger in relying on the Indian image as guardian of the rainforest. This image implies that Indian lifestyles should be given a chance to survive because of specific acts they perform that are beneficial to the environment, rather than basing the defense of indigenous rights on recognition of their rights to self-determination as a nation. (Fisher 1994: 229)

The Kayapó have become the most important economic group in their region, as neighboring Brazilians have become dependent on the proceeds of logging and mining in the Kayapó reserve. Around 70 per cent of the region's economic activity is related to these two industries. But the Kayapó's success has led to unprecedented problems for the group, their Brazilian neighbors and the environment (Rabben 1995).

The Downside of Development

In Gorotire, for example, gold mining seemed like a great deal at first. Goods and money rolled into the community, and the benefits were immediate. The health of the people improved, and a teacher came to give the children instruction. People built better houses. Generators provided electricity to every house.

But Gorotire village became dirty as a result of the presence of thousands of outsiders in the reserve. Mining was environmentally damaging, especially to the rivers and river banks where gold was extracted. The incidence of malaria and sexually transmitted diseases increased. Gorotire's residents cut short their traditional hunting and gathering treks and increasingly depended on purchased food. The focus of social life in the village shifted from men's age-sets to families and households. As the outside world massively impinged on the Kayapó, local leaders acquired sufficient knowledge and sophistication to represent their people on regional, national and even international levels. Young leaders, including Payakan, began spending more time in town, where they acquired a reputation for drinking, conspicuous consumption and womanising. Village life was strained by all these changes in the course of a decade.

By the early 1990s, disturbing phenomena, such as stillbirths and congenital birth defects, began to appear in Gorotire. With support from the Japanese Rainforest Foundation, Brazilian anthropologist Olimpio Serra assembled an interdisciplinary team to do research on the effects of mercury contamination on Gorotire residents. Mercury in the soil, on river bottoms, in food and in the air has contaminated vast areas of the Amazon basin as a result of widespread gold mining by hundreds of thousands of prospectors. The study found that the Gorotire Kayapó, their environment and the miners all showed signs of serious mercury contamination.

With the outsiders also came diseases, from tuberculosis to gonorrhea. One of the Kayapó's most pressing concerns was providing medical care in the villages, instead of flying sick people 100 miles to the nearest town. In 1993 the Rainforest Foundation sent a nurse to several communities to do a health survey. In Kubenkokre (population 480) she found a nurse, paid by FUNAI, who "uses medications to excess ... antibiotics [are] used indiscriminately, with no control of the dosage at the time of administration" (Machado 1993: 1). Basic equipment, such as thermometer and stethoscope, was lacking. The local diet was healthful, food abundant, but villagers made coffee from polluted river water. All the houses and the clinic had electricity, and some residents watched national news and soccer games on the television in the men's house.

Problems in Pukanu village included "precarious" medical and dental care, poorly trained health workers, excessive use of medication, poor record keeping, excessive expenditure on hospital care in town. These conditions are typical of those in many indigenous areas.

A year later, a physician made a follow-up visit to several Kayapó communities (Tanaka 1994). She found 53 abnormal Pap test results among 120 samples, and many cases of sexually transmitted diseases among women, whose husbands had apparently infected them. In Pukanu (population 250), 36 residents had malaria, probably as a result of their proximity to garimpeiros. The community cistern was contaminated.

The doctor noted that the Kayapó put "unbearable" pressure on the nurse in Kubenkokre to send patients to the hospital in town. The nurse, who was paid by a logging company, knuckled under because she feared losing her job.

Loyal Opposition

Not all Kayapó leaders wanted to keep making deals that brought disease to their communities, fouled the environment and allowed outsiders to deplete their patrimony. Raoni and some others represented an important sector of Kayapó public opinion, which saw breakneck development by outsiders as a threat to traditional culture. They also represented those who did not benefit from mining and logging, the proceeds of which were unequally distributed in the community. This sector of the Kayapó saw preservation of the traditional means of subsistence as more desirable than transitory gains that could have devastating long-term consequences, to people as well as to nature, the basis of their subsistence.

In 1993 a delegation of Kayapó leaders went to Brasília to lobby for permission to sell mahogany that logging companies had illegally cut. They also sought a continuation of federal government responsibility for their welfare (known as *tutela*, tutelage, in Brazilian law).

Also in 1993, the Attorney General's Office, an independent federal agency, filed a suit to remove all non-indigenous miners and loggers from the Kayapó Indigenous Area, on the grounds that they were plundering the environment and compromising the health of the Indians. Among the evidence was the interdisciplinary team's report on mercury contamination. The Federal District Court of Brasilia ordered the expulsion in February 1994. FUNAI had responsibility to carry out the order, but the agency, whose budget had been cut by 90 per cent in recent years, said it had no resources to do so (CIMI 1994d; FUNAI 1994).

Márcio Santilli, then working for NDI, a non-governmental organisation that provided legal assistance to indigenous groups, traveled to the Kayapó reserve soon after the court ruling came down. He observed that the situation in Gorotire was:

... difficult; food is scarcer and few fields have been planted ... the health situation is grave, and there is much tuberculosis, malaria and venereal disease ... the vehicles were broken, and there was no diesel to run the lighting system. The undergrowth had grown, even in the area of the infirmary and the school (closed for lack of a teacher). (NDI 1994: 3)

The Indians thought that the court had banned them, as well as outsiders, from mining or logging. Santilli explained that only non-indigenous miners and loggers had to stop working and that the environmental law prohibited the kind of work that destroys rivers and forests in any area, even on the lands of the whites. If the Indians decided to take over mining and do it differently, without mercury and with other environmental safeguards, the judge (and the law) did not forbid it.

The Kayapó leaders replied:

Someone has to be held responsible for everything that happened during the 12 years that they taught us the wrong way to work. Who will clean up the rivers and the forests that have been damaged? Who will be responsible for health care? Who will indemnify us for the resources and the lives we have lost? (NDI 1994: 3)

By September 1994, the Kayapó could wait no longer for an answer. Young warriors forcibly expelled about 2,000 non-indigenous miners still in the reserve. Under community pressure, older leaders supported their initiative. This alliance across generations outflanked the middle generation of leaders, who had tried to act as mediators between the Indians and Brazilian businessmen in Redenção. The miners fled to the city, where they occupied the main square and threatened to attack the FUNAI office and the Kayapó who were there. Eventually a gold buyer and the mayor negotiated an agreement, whereby the miners would return to Gorotire for six months. In exchange, the gold buyer would pay off the Kayapó's outstanding debts in Redenção, which then amounted to some $200,000. Several young leaders who had benefited from earlier mining and logging deals were primarily responsible for these debts, but the community as a whole agreed to the deal. Uneasy coexistence between the Kayapó and outsiders seemed re-established in Gorotire.

Nonetheless the Attorney General's office insisted on enforcing the expulsion order. And ordinary Kayapó, who have seen few benefits from the depredation of their natural patrimony, kept pressuring community leaders to go along with the federal government. In December 1994 the leaders agreed to support the expulsion of all non-indigenous miners from Kayapó territory for at least a year (Turner 1995b).

Open Questions

The issue resurfaced in late 1995, when a group of young leaders demanded that FUNAI pay their debts – which had allegedly swelled to $2 million – in Redenção. They occupied the local FUNAI office until a settlement could be worked out. Payakan, who had lost his environmental credentials by making deals with loggers, seems to have been involved in this action. How the Kayapó would finance their future development in a sustainable way, without selling off their patrimony, remained unsettled.

Meanwhile, leaders still living on the reserve were organising local associations, which had the legal capacity to seek funding for economic development projects from outside sources. One started an eco-tourism project, another an extractive-product project to provide alternatives to mining and logging. The local leaders operate in a traditional way, forming and managing groups of followers, but they seek to integrate the reserve into the local, regional and national economies.

The Kayapó "have modified many aspects of their village life, social organisation and surroundings in the process of surviving more than 200 years of colonial and post-colonial onslaughts"

(Fisher 1994: 229). They do not live in perfect harmony with pristine nature; indigenous peoples, like other human beings, have always affected their environments, sometimes positively, sometimes negatively. Like the rest of us, they must continually make choices about their relationship to nature, which is never static or simple.

Meanwhile, in Gorotire ...

On a visit to Gorotire in September 1997, I found some of the same problems Santilli had reported in 1994. The generator still sat idle for lack of diesel fuel. The village was extremely dirty, the river polluted. Villagers depended increasingly on food trucked in from Redenção. Corroding batteries littered the ground where children played. The hospital was abandoned, its screens torn, its bathroom filthy. A nurse had left a couple of months earlier and had not been replaced. There were no drugs in the infirmary. Someone had sabotaged the village water supply, and the water storage towers were empty.

With a Brazilian engineer who the village *cacique* (headman) paid to fix such problems, I climbed a nearby hill to the reservoir, a lovely, secluded pool near the summit. Someone had removed the filter cap from the main pipe feeding water to the village, and twigs, leaves and branches had blocked the pipe. The engineer and a couple of helpers took about an hour to locate the blockages and clear them. They replaced the filter (which the saboteur had con-siderately left a few feet from the pipe), and we descended to the *cerrado* (plain).

Back at the village, water was still not flowing to the school, which the county council administers. The engineer started digging holes to see where the problem might be. Over the village loudspeaker, the cacique's wife asked for help from the men of the village, but only one man responded to her plea. The others were out hunting turtles for an upcoming festival or did not choose to help. The engineer finally found the place where a pipe had to be replaced. School was cancelled so the two teachers could help him with the work.

The cacique pays the engineer for his services out of the money he receives from loggers who are extracting mahogany from the reserve. Although the Brazilian government announced with great fanfare in 1996 that mahogany exports would be banned for two years, this proclamation does not seem to have slowed logging on indigenous land, where most of the mahogany is located.

Since the Kayapó expelled the miners in 1995, the cacique observed, the situation has worsened in Gorotire, because now FUNAI does nothing for them and they do not gain anything from the few miners who remain in the reserve. He hopes to obtain government approval for a project that would train the Kayapó to mine gold without using mercury or devastating the environment. But the government moves slowly at the best of times, and in Brasilia all the talk was about a bill moving swiftly through Congress that would give mining companies freer access to indigenous lands. The results of granting such access, either through neglect or design, have already been seen in Yanomami territory and in Gorotire: pollution, destruction, disease, violence, death.

In Gorotire, the largest Kayapó village and the one most affected by contact with Brazilian society, the Kayapó have not yet found a way to sustainably develop their territory and equitably distribute the benefits of civilisation. Instead, a two-class system, with a small elite that benefits from development and a majority that does not, is evolving in imitation of the Brazilian system that surrounds it.

Some of the more remote Kayapó villages, especially those west of the Xingu River, have managed to escape or prevent such depredation by refusing to make deals with loggers and miners. They are trying to develop eco-tourism or sustainable extraction of nuts, fruit and other forest products.

And the next time the Brazilian government proposes a hydroelectric project, highway or other mega-project that threatens Kayapó sovereignty (as it is sure to do), the Kayapó leaders will meet to take action, and Tu'ire and her relatives will prepare their weapons.

Two decades ago, Turner observed:

> Given half a chance, indigenous groups can make a successful and vital adaptation to contact with Brazilian society. The indigenous societies of Amazonia and their cultures are not doomed to disappear: on the contrary, many, like the Kayapó, show strong signs of being on the way to more or less viable forms of accommodation with Brazilian society without losing either their social or political cohesion as internally self-governing communities or the essential elements of their own culture. (Turner 1978: 21)

Actors now on regional, national and world stages, the Kayapó keep facing new challenges in dealing with the outside world and with one another. Since the mid-1980s they have shown themselves to be resourceful and clever participants in Brazilian public affairs, as allies or enemies, depending on how they define and redefine their own interests. Their apparent success at transcending internal divisions and protecting their cultural patrimony has made them an attractive model for Brazil's other indigenous peoples, who are struggling to survive. But the Kayapó pay a price for this success, and they must keep confronting its consequences.

Paulinho Payakan at Altamira, 1989.
Photo by Eduardo Leão, Conselho Indigenista Missionário.

4

Payakan: A Cautionary Tale

Hundreds of Brazilian Indians attended the 1992 international indigenous conference in Rio, but one of their most famous and brilliant activists was not there. Paulinho Payakan, the Kayapó warrior whose serious face had recently appeared under the headline, "The Man Who Would Save the World," on the cover of a popular US magazine, was expected but never arrived. Nor did he attend the Earth Summit that followed.

Since 1988, Payakan had led the struggle to defend indigenous interests in Brazil and beyond. Almost every month, it seemed, he was traveling to one capital or another, organising a meeting, giving interviews, leading a delegation. He was one of a few Brazilian Indians whose faces became familiar to international audiences.

So where was Payakan in mid-1992? His absence from the conference seemed to lessen its importance. There was something ominous in other Indians' reluctance to talk about him. Then came the headlines and the elemental shock of scandal.

Great struggles breed stars: charismatic characters who embody the causes for which they fight. In the age of mass communication, we know their faces, their voices and their words as if they were our neighbors, instead of remote figures at the other end of the world. At the same time, we want them to be exotic and colorful. Furthermore, we expect them to transcend the circumstances that forced them to fight. They parade like mythological creatures or personifications of virtue on the world stage. But these larger-than-life figures sometimes fail. At those times the public becomes implacable, overturning the pedestal we built and slamming the hapless hero down to our own level, or even below.

The struggles of indigenous peoples for survival (or for something more than mere survival) have made international stars of people drastically different from their audiences. They have had to learn much more about us than we care to know about them. Indigenous activists like Payakan, Raoni and Davi Yanomami, who toured the world in the 1980s warning of environmental disasters, had to translate their reality into terms the international public could understand. Seduced by their eloquence and their powerful physical presence, we made extravagant offers of help and then sent them home, sometimes with their pockets full of money, other times empty-handed.

In the meantime, the dangers they denounced continued to threaten their people. On their return to the forest, these leaders had to face local reality. But we were no longer interested; some other heroic figure had taken their place in our imaginations.

Despite our fickleness, indigenous leaders still felt obliged to realise the promises of immediate improvement they had made to their people. These promises were ultimately what had sent them to faraway desinations and then brought them back home.

Returning from stardom could be painful and difficult. Often the leaders could satisfy neither the expectations of the outside world nor of their own communities. They were left hanging amidst multiple worlds and multiple demands.

The story of Payakan – defender of the Amazon rainforest, Kayapó ambassador to the First World, dreamer, community organiser, deal maker, profiteer, possible rapist – includes all these elements. He began as a shooting star and ended as a falling one. Following his trajectory were outside supporters and allies who became too emotionally involved in their ideal of the struggle to back away. To some of them, Payakan seemed like his own worst enemy, but other antagonists were not lacking, either.

After the Fall

Three years after his disappearance from the international scene, Payakan moved restlessly between the Kayapó reserve in central Brazil and the rough frontier town of Redenção ("Redemption"). Many of his supporters on the reserve had moved away from him, and his ideas for developing his community seemed more like illusions than dreams. In the international arena, he was largely forgotten.

A few sympathetic people still tried to help him. Canadian biologist Barbara Zimmerman, who runs an ecological research station near his home village of A'ukre, kept him on her payroll. On a steamy afternoon in November 1995, she was beginning a two-day journey home to Toronto after four months in a Kayapó village. She made a strangely glamorous impression as she waited in the tiny airport of Redenção. Traces of body paint stained her shins, above serviceable Timberlands and just below the hem of a fashionably long cotton dress. She chatted with Payakan as she waited for the small plane that would take her to Brasilia.

A few minutes after her arrival, Márcio Santilli, the embattled President of FUNAI, checked in. He was on his way back to Brasilia after difficult negotiations with Kayapó warriors who had invaded the FUNAI office in Redenção and taken several hostages. Santilli's mobile face looked miserable, as if he were asking himself, "Why on earth did I take this job?"

Three months later, 20 Xavante warriors armed with clubs would storm his office in Brasilia, force him into the building's underground garage and harangue him for an hour, thrusting their forefingers in his face, demanding immediate assistance for their people. All he could tell them was that the Congress had not yet passed FUNAI's appropriation, and the agency had no money to spend on the Xavante or any other indigenous group.[1] Santilli resigned in March 1996.

Some Kayapó leaders in Redenção were also demanding money, to pay an estimated $2 million debt they had run up in the town while buying everything from cases of Coca-Cola to ship to their villages, to the services of local prostitutes. They claimed they had spent most of the money hiring planes to send sick relatives from the reserve to hospitals for emergency medical treatment. They had to do this, they told the media, because FUNAI was not carrying out its statutory responsibilities, which included providing schooling, medical assistance, infrastructure and environmental protection to 14 Kayapó communities in three reserves. Therefore, they said, FUNAI should pay the debt.

Santilli flew 600 miles to Redenção to tell the Kayapó warriors that FUNAI auditors would look into the matter. The Indians let the FUNAI workers go but kept the office administrator hostage in a Kayapó village. Three months later, he was still there.

The Kayapó used these highly visible strong-arm tactics time and again against Brazilian federal officials because they worked. As if going to war, they would paint themselves, put on feather and bead decorations, heft their heavy wooden clubs and shoulder their video cameras. Government officials almost always blinked first. Payakan was often involved (or behind) these dramatic sorties.

Barbara Zimmerman saw another side of him and the Kayapó during four years as the director of Conservation International's ecological research station near A'ukre. Leaving her husband and three children in Toronto, she would stay in A'ukre for weeks at a time, living as the Kayapó did, during four-month stints in Brazil. "It's tough physically, it's tough in every way," she said.

The Kayapó, she noted, "are really open to any new idea." They are very intelligent, and "if you explain something to them, they understand it" and are eager to try it. One village wanted to start an eco-tourism project but didn't know how to manage it. Zimmerman was looking for funding and people, "mature people, with some experience" of Brazil, to operate it. Back in Toronto, she seemed to find fund raising and proposal writing more daunting than weeks in the bush. Funders, she complained, "don't have any idea of what Indians are really like" (interview with author Feb. 1996).

No sooner did Zimmerman arrive in A'ukre for the first time in 1992 than she had to confront a crisis. The village was split by personal rivalries and conflicts centered on Payakan. He had persuaded the Body Shop to set up a pioneering extractive project in A'ukre.[2] Although this triumph gave him great prestige, his allegedly authoritarian ways stirred up opposition in the village.

Anthropologists who have studied the Kayapó point out that internal divisions are common among them. In the old days, villages split as a result of fights over women or ceremonial practices; now the fights focus on money: who gets it, who gives it away, who spends it, on what. Up and coming leaders gain prestige by bringing goods back from the outside world and distributing them to the community. Thus the shipments of Coca-Cola – bought with money obtained through deals with loggers and miners, who extracted gold and mahogany from Kayapó lands and paid a percentage of the proceeds to Kayapó leaders, including Payakan.

It was said he gave jobs and goods only to his close relatives. Other community members felt left out and resentful. Among many indigenous societies, stinginess is the greatest sin, and accumulation of goods is praiseworthy only in so far as it leads to equitable distribution.

When Zimmerman arrived in A'ukre to direct the new research station, she faced an angry crowd who complained about Payakan's control over the resources that had come into the village through the Body Shop project. To her the solution seemed obvious: a council of village men and women to oversee the project. But more dramatic developments made the council superfluous; the village split and about half the population moved away. Payakan's control was re-established.

Zimmerman learned how to work with Payakan and the Kayapó through trial and error. "The first year I really screwed up," she recalled, by giving money to the Kayapó leader who ran the local FUNAI post. Community members told her never to do that again.

Afterwards she sought written authorisation from as many community members as possible for every decision she took on behalf of the village.

Because money was coming into A'ukre, some of the disaffected villagers drifted back over time. In 1995, however, the community once again split. Again, conflict centered on Payakan. More than half the villagers, who did not believe they were benefiting from the Body Shop project, left, this time apparently for good, and set up another village downriver. Two such splits during a three-year period showed, Zimmerman thought, that Payakan is a particularly problematic figure for his own people.

Brazilians also have found him difficult and compelling. During the Kayapó takeover of the FUNAI office in Redenção, from behind the scenes he advised the young warriors who carried out the invasion. In the outside world he was fatally compromised by the rape charge that made international headlines at the time of the Earth Summit in 1992. Nevertheless, Brazilian television reporters went to Redenção to interview him during the takeover, more than three years later. There is something about Payakan that still forces whites and Indians to pay attention.

Physically, he has none of the exotic allure of his older kinsman, Raoni, who also became internationally famous during the 1980s, when he toured the world with Sting. A large, powerful man, Raoni has a commanding presence, reinforced by the prominent wooden lip plate he always wears in public. Raoni seems a true representative of the "Fourth World," an ambassador from another reality. Payakan is smaller, though stocky enough to be physically imposing on occasion. Unprepossessing, he has often been photographed with an unsmiling, almost uneasy, expression. After the rape charge, Brazil's major news magazine plastered his glum face on its cover, above the words, "The Savage."

In contrast, Payakan looked at ease and seemed in good spirits as he sat with Barbara Zimmerman in Redenção airport in November 1995. Dressed in casual Brazilian style, he chatted and joked with other Kayapó leaders, Santilli and the mayor of Redenção. After Zimmerman and Santilli left, he went off with his age-mates and the mayor for lunch in town.

Payakan at Home

Arranging an interview with Payakan was not easy. He kept postponing the meeting time or not answering the telephone. His wife would pick up the receiver and start speaking in Kayapó, or another member of the household would come on the line and say Payakan was away, then turn to him and ask him what to say next. Finally a meeting was set for the next day.

Payakan lives in an ordinary-looking but large stucco house on an unpaved street in Redenção. Like his house, most of the town has the raw, unfinished look of the frontier. When I arrived to interview him, he was standing in front of a camera, giving an interview to a TV reporter on the takeover of the FUNAI office. His manner was assured and friendly, his statement brief but articulate. He clearly has considerable experience at presenting himself as a spokesman for his people.

But he could not give the scheduled interview; apologetically he said he had to go to the FUNAI office to talk to the Kayapó warriors still occupying it. How about later in the afternoon?

At four o'clock, as the light faded slowly from the brilliant blue sky, he greeted visitors at his house. A few Kayapó women and children sat on the courtyard pavement and stared. The house was crudely finished, with little furniture; it looked almost unoccupied. The rooms were large and dark, and there was a sadness about the place. Payakan's office contained a desk, two chairs, a couple of tables, a shortwave radio, a generator and other equipment.

Payakan was unwelcoming, resistant, almost hostile. He sat behind the desk, fiddling with a pencil. Having talked many times about his early life with journalists from Europe, the US and Japan, he did not want to answer questions about it. There was a long silence.

Almost defiantly he said, "The struggle I've waged has been my own, not for all the Kayapó; it was a struggle that I sought. Nowadays I'm at the disposal of the Kayapó people. If they want me to act, I will. If they don't want me, that's it."

Asked if he would choose to fight the same battles again, he answered no. "It was worth the effort, it was good. I wanted to do it, and I did it. I don't want to do it any more ... I've had enough, I don't have the desire any more."

Nevertheless, he described himself as "part of a group that has the capacity to lead the people," but he had learned that leading doesn't mean telling people what to do. And he said he was "someone who observes and analyzes," a surprising self-characterisation from a man known, for better or worse, for his actions. After this revelation, the unsmiling visage in the news photographs made more sense. Perhaps his expression had not expressed unease, but the concentration of a man trying to figure things out and keep on top of them as they happened, in languages and cultures utterly alien from his own.

He blamed whites for the occupation of the FUNAI office.

This crisis isn't the Indian's fault, but the whites'. They taught us wrong, and FUNAI itself didn't bother to guide or teach the Kayapó so they could cope with white society. We've realised that the whites taught us to get money but didn't teach us how to spend or use it. There's still time to teach, and that's why we are preparing ourselves to help our people. Dependence on whites will never help. (interview with author Nov. 1995)

Oddly, this sounded like what Márcio Santilli had said in an interview a few days before, and what he would say three months hence to the angry Xavante who surrounded him in FUNAI's underground garage. Indigenous people have to come up with their own sustainable development projects, Santilli told them; the era of white paternalism is over.

Between Two Worlds

Despite his declaration of independence, Payakan depends on whites for his subsistence. According to Barbara Zimmerman, "He's nobly trying to put his three girls through school" in Redenção. He pays tuition out of his salaries from FUNAI and Zimmerman's project. He told me:

The important thing is for the Indian to keep being an Indian, to know his culture. If the Indian doesn't maintain his culture, doesn't know it, forgets and goes to the city to live like whites, doesn't want to be an Indian or know about his people, doesn't fight for indigenous rights, then you can say he doesn't care about Indians. (interview with author Nov. 1995)

Although he said he was moving slowly back to the reserve to live, he seemed to see his daughters' future in the white world, not in the forest.

Rumors about his fabulous wealth, his cars and airplanes, seem extremely exaggerated. Zimmerman's housekeeper insisted that "he isn't in any kind of need," but the cupboards and refrigerator in his house were almost bare. Payakan's control over large sums of money from loggers or the Body Shop ended sometime after the

1992 rape charge terminated his career as an international celebrity, though he continued to make deals with loggers. It remains to be seen if he will manage to raise funds for his current project, the grandiosely named "University of Kayapó Culture," a maloca without walls next to an airstrip in a remote corner of the reserve.

Barbara Zimmerman, who said, "I probably know him as well as anybody can," described Payakan's character as "incredibly complex." Sometimes he seems "manic," with lots of good ideas, "but he has trouble focusing" and lacks the capacity or training to execute or administer projects. Within his community, however, he is "a powerful character" (interview with author Feb. 1996). What happened to the man who organised the 1989 Altamira meeting and many other actions with considerable administrative skill?

Payakan has been a Kayapó leader since the early 1980s, and the ups and downs of his career parallel the indigenous group's adventurous experiments with modernisation. Most of the Kayapó have been in "peaceful" contact with Brazilian society since 1950. Nonetheless, they have not hesitated to defend themselves or attack outsiders when necessary.

The Kayapó suffered the devastating consequences of epidemics, invasions, conflicts and other insults that predatory outsiders inflicted on them. But unlike many other Brazilian indigenous groups, Kayapó culture did not collapse or disappear under the assaults of civilisation. Despite their internal divisions, they have consistently managed to close ranks against external threats to their survival as a people. Moreover, they have taken audacious actions to ensure their vitality and prosperity. During the past decade Payakan has often organised or led these initiatives.

Life on the Edge

Payakan was born in 1955 in the village of Kubenkranken. Curious, intelligent and enterprising, he learned Portuguese from the outsiders who came to the village as teachers, missionaries, researchers and FUNAI officials. As a youth he worked on a road construction crew, where he gained experience in the ways of ordinary Brazilians.

Payakan grew up during a period when increasing numbers of whites were entering Kayapó territory to extract natural resources or seize land for their own uses (cattle ranching, homesteading, hunting). Famed and feared for their bellicosity, the Kayapó reacted with carefully measured violence. According to Turner, "Perhaps 30 settlers, ranchers and other [invaders] ... were killed by Kayapó between 1970 and 1990, and many others were driven off by armed attacks" (Turner 1995b: 13).

At the same time, some Kayapó leaders were making deals with loggers and miners in exchange for money and improvements such as roads, houses and other buildings. The most famous was Tut Pombo, who, Turner says, "became the prototype ... emulated by several Kayapó leaders of the next generation, who used their command of Portuguese and familiarity with Brazilian ways as a base of political influence" (Turner 1995b: 15).

When he was a boy in the 1930s, Pombo (whose name in Kayapó and Portuguese means "dove") survived a massacre by Brazilians that killed the rest of his family. He was taken to a nearby city and raised in a Brazilian household, where he learned to speak Portuguese. As a young man he returned to Gorotire, and the Indian protection agency named him village "chief" because of his language ability. In 1976 he founded his own village, Kikretum. When gold miners started working near the village without his permission, he raided their camp and expelled them. But later he became the first Kayapó leader to offer concessions to gold miners and mahogany loggers. With the proceeds, he built Brazilian-style houses for the community and bought an airplane, houses and a hotel in the city of Tucumã, where he lived in high style. He died of natural causes in 1992 (Ricardo 1996: 420–1).

In the late 1970s and early 1980s, as the world price of gold surged up to $850 an ounce, gold was discovered in several parts of the Amazon region. The huge open-pit mine of Serra Pelada, not far from Kayapó territory, attracted tens of thousands of prospectors. The spillover flowed into indigenous areas. Although such mining was illegal, the government condoned it "as a social safety valve, to divert and diffuse the acute social tensions in the region" (Turner 1995b: 14).

Two mining sites opened in 1981 near Gorotire, whose leaders made a deal with mining entrepreneurs to receive a percentage of the profits. The mining company cheated the Kayapó by agreeing to give them 10 per cent of the proceeds and then moving the decimal point in the contract from 0.1 to 0.001. Not knowing enough arithmetic to perceive the trick, the Kayapó signed the contract. Soon 5,000 miners were mining gold near Gorotire under military supervision.

The Go-betweens

Payakan understood Brazilian culture well enough to oppose the deal. As FUNAI's "chief of post" at Gorotire, he negotiated a contract slightly more favorable to the Kayapó and deposited the proceeds in a community bank account in the city. Two other young leaders – like Payakan, sons of senior chiefs – took over administration of the deal. They moved the profits to bank accounts in their fathers' names, thus keeping the money under their own control and turning their fathers into figureheads.

Payakan lost prestige as a result of his rivals' maneuvers. FUNAI moved him to its regional office in Belém. "From this vantage point," notes Turner, "he coordinated the confrontation of the Gorotire with the company running the gold mines . . . when its contract with the Gorotire came up for renewal in 1985" (Turner 1995a: 52). On behalf of the Kayapó, FUNAI asked the company for a 10 per cent share, but the company balked. Payakan organised (by two-way radio) an attack by 200 warriors from Gorotire and Kikretum, who seized the airstrip and equipment at one of the mine sites and prevented planes from bringing in supplies.

The Kayapó became national news at this point. They demanded that the federal government intervene on their behalf. In exchange for allowing the miners to continue working, the Indians would control mine operations and collect 10 per cent of the proceeds – and the government would recognise their rights to their territory by demarcating their reserve.

Astonished by this challenge, the government sent troops, plus a military band that paraded along the airstrip "in a ludicrous and unsuccessful attempt to intimidate the Kayapó" (Turner 1995a: 52). Although the company succeeded in reducing the Kayapó's share to 5 per cent, the Indians gained control over both mining and demarcation. It was Payakan who negotiated for them in Belém and Brasilia.

Brazil's first civilian government in 21 years demarcated a reserve of more than 3 million hectares for the Kayapó. The Indians themselves supervised mining, prevented smuggling and patrolled their frontiers. "Within a year, invasions effectively ceased" (Turner 1990: 14).

A relatively small number of young, Portuguese-speaking Kayapó leaders, including Payakan, became prominent as a result of the brilliantly coordinated actions of 1985. They imitated Pombo by living in the town of Redenção, where "they acquired cars, trucks, airplanes, Brazilian servants" while the miners extracted millions of dollars in gold every year (Turner 1995b: 16). Thus, Payakan and his age-mates became members of the regional elite. The economy of southern Pará state became dependent on Kayapó resources. A Redenção bank manager conservatively estimated that gross profits from mining and logging on the three Kayapó reserves came to $10 million a year, of which the Indians received about $1.5 million. Suddenly the Kayapó were the richest indigenous group in Brazil. Their political power soared.

In 1986, the federal government tried to dump radioactive waste from the nuclear accident in Goiânia on the Kayapó's western frontier. One-hundred warriors flew to Brasília to demonstrate and the dumping plan was abandoned.

In 1987, 50 Kayapó representatives were frequently photographed and interviewed as they attended sessions, gave press conferences and lobbied at the Constitutional Convention in Brasília. Several Brazilian NGOs advised and collaborated with them to ensure passage of provisions that strengthened indigenous rights.

The Environment Heats Up

The Kayapó came to the First World's attention in 1988, after two hot, dry summers in the First World that fanned concern (if not hysteria) about global warming. Payakan and other leaders got wind of ambitious government plans to build ten dams along major Amazon rivers, including the Xingu. Three of the projects would flood large parts of Kayapó territory.

Payakan and his age-mate Kuben-I, who has often competed with him for political and economic power, were invited to an environmental conference in Miami by anthropologist Janet Chernela. On this, their first trip out of Brazil, accompanied by anthropologist Darrell Posey (who studied the Kayapó for many years), they denounced the hydroelectric projects. After the conference they went with Posey and Chernela to Washington, DC, where they met with officials of the World Bank, which was to finance the dams. At the Bank they obtained detailed information about the project that the Brazilian government was trying to keep secret from its own citizens.

Soon after their return to Brazil, Payakan, Kuben-I and Posey were indicted under the Foreigners Law, which forbids aliens from involving themselves in political activities in Brazil. The absurdity of prosecuting indigenous people under this law was immediately obvious. Posey, who lived in Belém and taught at a federal university, was in real trouble, however – despite the fact that he had assisted the Indians while in his own country. During the summer of 1988, he was ostentatiously followed by federal agents and his telephone was tapped. His position at the university became untenable.

Anthropologists, indigenous rights advocates and human rights organisations around the world leapt to the men's defense. The Brazilian government began to look foolish.

Early in 1989 Payakan and Kuben-I were summoned to Belém for arraignment. They arrived at the courthouse with 500 Kayapó supporters. As Turner (1990: 16) tells it:

> Kayapó men and women danced through the streets and massed in the square before the Palace of Justice ... Kayapó orators unrolled the map of the Xingu dam scheme obtained from the World Bank in Washington on an easel erected in the square and explained the entire secret project in Kayapó and Portuguese for the benefit of the many Brazilian onlookers, who included reporters and TV crews.

Photos of Kayapó warriors, painted for battle and carrying war clubs, arrayed against police and troops, appeared on front pages around the world.

Inside the courtroom, Payakan and Kuben-I presented themselves to the judge, who took umbrage at their colorful appearance. He declared that their body paint, feather and bead ornaments and swimming trunks were not proper attire and showed disrespect for the court. The Indians objected that they were wearing their best ceremonial garb.

Enraged, the judge ruled that an anthropologist would have to be contracted to determine if the Indians were sufficiently acculturated to understand the charges against them. But no anthropologist could be found to take on the assignment. Soon after, the charges against Payakan and Kuben-I were quietly dropped. Posey later left Brazil and has not lived there since.

Spectacle at Altamira

At the time of the arraignment Payakan was already busy with a project that was to bring him and the Kayapó lasting international fame. With the help of CEDI, a Brazilian NGO, he was organising a pan-indigenous meeting to protest the Xingu dam projects and confront Brazilian officials who were still refusing to release information about the plans. The place was Altamira, a frontier town not far from the northern boundaries of the Kayapó reserve. Payakan invited not only high-ranking Brazilian officials but hundreds of indigenous people, including 500 Kayapó, Brazilian and international NGO representatives, parliamentarians and journalists – about 1,200 people in all. It was "an impressive feat of organisational and political coordination" (Turner 1990: 19).

At the meeting site the Kayapó built a model village, as if they were on one of their seasonal treks. They prepared for a traditional ritual, the New Corn Ceremony, which they performed during the five-day meeting. Payakan had no trouble executing or administering his ideas on this occasion, though he did suddenly fall ill with appendicitis. He underwent emergency surgery and showed up, shaky but triumphant, at Altamira a couple of days late. In a moving traditional greeting, the Kayapó burst into tears as he entered the model village.

Despite strong Brazilian opposition to the meeting, it went off without violent incidents – thanks, Turner thought, to Kayapó self-discipline and the massive presence of the international media. Perhaps because the meeting happened only a few weeks after the assassination of Chico Mendes, neither the government nor local landowners and merchants who supported the dam projects had the heart to make trouble. Perhaps they also knew too well the fierce reputation of the Kayapó.

What violence did occur was symbolic. In an incident relayed around the world, Tu'ire, a young Kayapó, strode up to the podium while the director of the regional electric-power authority was explaining the Xingu projects. Deliberately she placed the side of her machete on the director's cheek and made a brief oration in Kayapó as he sat there trembling. It was an electrifying moment.

The meeting became an "international media circus" as famous personalities dropped in. Sting, who had recently raised more than $1 million for Kayapó demarcation on worldwide tour with Raoni, came for one day to promote his project. The arrival of Raoni, at that moment perhaps the most famous indigenous person in the world, aroused great excitement among both indigenous participants and journalists.

More important, the Altamira meeting generated "serious political pressure against any international funding of the dam scheme" (Turner 1990: 20). Just two weeks later the World Bank announced that it would not lend the Brazilian government any funds for the Xingu project. The dams remain on the drawing board to this day, though the Brazilian government is again seeking international funding for them, this time from the private sector.

Even if Payakan had done or would do nothing else, his brilliant work on the Altamira meeting – and its results – would assure him a place in indigenous history.

Man of the World

During the late 1980s Brazil and the Amazon received unprecedented international attention. As a result, Payakan became a world traveler, meeting with environmentalists, scientists, parliamentarians, indigenous solidarity groups and the public in many countries. The North saw him as a defender of the Amazon rainforest, but Payakan was defending Kayapó interests. The two roles did not necessarily coincide or cohere. Payakan had a keenly pragmatic sense of how to reconcile the differing perspectives and groups to whom he spoke during his travels, however. In a speech at the University of Chicago in 1988, he said:

> The forest is one big thing; it has people, animals and plants. There is no point saving the animals if the forest is burned down; there is no point saving the forest if the people and animals who live in it are killed or driven away. The groups trying to save the races of animals cannot win if the people trying to save the forest lose; the people trying to save the Indians cannot win if either of the others lose; the Indians cannot win without the support of these groups; but the groups cannot win either without the support of the Indians, who know the forest and the animals and can tell what is happening to them. No one of us is strong enough to win alone; together, we can be strong enough to win. (Turner 1990: 18)

With this discourse he helped build coalitions and secure alliances that would benefit the Kayapó and himself. Furthermore, he showed that "the supposedly hapless victims of progress have assumed a leading role" in preserving both the environment and themselves (Turner 1990: 22). Payakan surprised Northerners, accustomed to seeing indigenous peoples as doomed atavists, by demonstrating that the Kayapó had taken their fate into their own hands. Thus he countered "the hopelessness induced by apocalyptic but often inaccurate news stories of 'genocide' and widespread romantic cliches like the inevitable disappearance of primitive peoples in the path of progress," Turner pointed out. By promoting specific projects such as his "Mebengokre Foundation," Payakan encouraged Northern supporters to invest in the Kayapó financially as well as emotionally.

In 1995, Payakan made a modest and astute assessment of his travels.

> It didn't result in much for the Kayapó, though it helped Brazilian Indians in general. During the period when I was taking the Kayapó to the city and traveling outside Brazil, the Kayapó were living well, off mining and logging money. But at the same time I was saying in the name of the Kayapó that my people were fighting on behalf of nature. And later, everybody was against what the Kayapó were doing. That's why I say that my trips outside Brazil and the image I presented of the Kayapó didn't bring results for the Kayapó but rather for Brazilian Indians. (interview with author Nov. 1995)

As a result of his international fame, in the early 1990s Payakan was riding high – perhaps too high for his constituency back in A'ukre, which demanded material gains and improvements in the short term. Other village leaders had already allowed loggers to extract mahogany from forests near the village. Payakan told Turner that although he opposed logging, he had realised it was inevitable and "decided to make deals on the best terms possible for the community" (Turner 1992b: 6). He used the proceeds to build houses and pipe in water from a nearby stream. But he insisted on keeping control, "convinced that only he knew how to make best use of the money" (1992b: 6). Conflicts with his rivals followed.

One of them told Turner that in 1990 Payakan made a deal worth about $40 million in timber, for which he received a one-time, 10 per cent payment of $392,000. His rival claimed that Payakan was skimming a large monthly sum for himself "without spending a penny on the community." The following year, he forced the rival out of the village so he could continue as sole intermediary to the loggers.

Payakan was not the only Kayapó leader to act in this way. His age-mates also made deals with loggers and miners and pocketed much of the proceeds. Beginning in 1990, reports reached the outside world that the Kayapó "were in effect acting as collaborators and profiteers in the destruction of their own forests and

rivers" (Turner 1992b: 12). In two years they had turned from ecological heroes into villains. International interest and support
gradually shifted to other indigenous groups and the upcoming
United Nations Conference on Environment and Development
(UNCED).

The Road Downhill

In 1991 Payakan's wife, Irekran, went to the doctor in Redenção
after suffering a miscarriage. Payakan later charged that the doctor
had sterilised her without her knowledge or consent, and he took
the highly unusual step (in the Brazilian context) of suing the
doctor. Saying that Payakan's status as a Kayapó leader was threatened because he had no male offspring, non-indigenous friends
raised funds for an expensive operation to reverse the sterilisation.
Although the operation was declared successful, Payakan and his
wife have had no more children. Payakan clearly saw this incident
as a deliberate attempt to sabotage him, and his mistrust of whites
seemed to increase.

Payakan was not to be seen at the UNCED preparatory conferences in 1991. When he appeared in Brasilia at meetings of the
Rainforest Foundation board (of which he was a member), he
seemed fretful, even self-pitying. In elaborate fits of pique, he
would ritualistically resign from the board at every meeting.
Finally the Foundation accepted his resignation.

At the Kari-Oca International Indigenous Conference, which
preceded UNCED in late May 1992, indigenous advocates asked
one another where Payakan was. Kayapó who did attend said only
that he was back in A'ukre; perhaps he would arrive later.

A few days later news of the rape charge broke as an exclusive
story in the weekly magazine *Veja*. The article was a hatchet job,
riddled with inaccuracies and permeated by racist assumptions,
clearly aimed at discrediting not only Payakan but the cause of
indigenous rights. The source of the "information" in the piece
was someone in the office of Pará's governor, who was suing the
federal government to repeal the demarcation of the Mekragnoti
Kayapó reserve. Surely it was not coincidental that the report
appeared a few days before the beginning of the Earth Summit.

A reporter and cameraman from TV Globo, Brazil's biggest
network, went to A'ukre to interview Payakan. On nationwide
television he seemed to admit his guilt: "Yes, I did it," he said,
looking sheepish, "but I can't remember it because I was drunk."

Supporters who rushed to his defense claimed Payakan had never admitted to rape; the footage had been cut to take his words out of context, they said.

Eighteen-year-old Silvia Ferreira, the alleged victim, told a sordid story: after a marathon party at a farmhouse outside Redenção, Payakan and Irekran gave her a ride home in Payakan's car. All three were extremely drunk. Payakan stopped the car, jumped into the back seat and assaulted Silvia with Irekran's assistance. Bloody and dazed, Silvia finally managed to escape. Two Brazilians, who happened to be nearby, rescued her as Payakan was trying to throttle her.

According to the *Veja* story, several days later Silvia underwent a forensic examination at the local hospital, and Payakan's semen was found on her underwear. Any rape victim's advocate (or a rape victim who has undergone such an exam) would find this part of the tale hard to believe. A forensic examination for rape is a painstaking procedure with an elaborate protocol, requiring special equipment, and it must be done within 48 hours of the crime. In order to determine whose semen is present, a DNA sample must be taken from the alleged perpetrator and tested. There is no indication that Payakan's blood or semen was tested, or that a forensic report was filed. And would a small hospital in a frontier town in the Amazon have the capability to carry out these procedures?

The *Veja* story also claimed that the inside of Payakan's car was stained with Silvia's blood. American journalist Scott Wallace went to Redenção a few weeks later and found the car. It had already been sold without the police examining it for evidence and was completely clean. As a result of this and other discoveries, Wallace doubted that a rape had occurred; in any event, the legal case against Payakan was weak. More than two years later, a judge threw out the case for lack of evidence.

On the other hand, rape victim advocates know from experience – and recent scientific literature on rape confirms – that most rape victims tell the truth. Silvia Ferreira probably did suffer some kind of violent assault in the back of Payakan's car. Whether or not Payakan's statement was taken out of context, he did admit that something had happened. It is possible that Irekran did most of the attacking. Under Brazilian law, however, she was considered an "unacculturated Indian" with insufficient understanding to be charged.

Turner visited the Kayapó soon after the rape charge was made and reported:

The Kayapó with whom I spoke in A'ukre, Gorotire and Kubenkranken accept that Payakan and his wife Irekran did something bad to the girl who accuses them. They think that the couple had drunk too much (Irekran more than Payakan), Payakan was messing around sexually with the girl, and Irekran attacked her, scratching her genital area and other parts of her body. The majority is doubtful whether rape or even intercourse occurred, remaining skeptical about the details ... The Kayapó are much more concerned about the reaction of the whites ... There was unanimous agreement that white reaction in general, and specifically that of the media, was excessive, far beyond what Payakan's actions deserved ... Despite their disapproval of his actions, the Kayapó with whom I spoke were disposed to defend him as a "relative" against the whites, because they saw the accusations ... as expressions of hostility toward them in general, motivated by the greed of some whites for their lands and resources. (Turner 1992b: 1)

If the intent of the rape charge was to bring Payakan down, it succeeded. Some Brazilian and international supporters defended him publicly and called the charge a sham, while others repeated the rumors of his deals with loggers and his high life in town, as if they proved his guilt. Payakan became a liability to the indigenous cause and an unreliable ally for environmentalists. Funders of sustainable development projects lost interest in financing his initiatives. Within his community, he retained some power and prestige, but significant opposition developed against him in A'ukre, leading to the splits that Barbara Zimmerman witnessed.

In Retrospect

In 1995 Payakan portrayed his retreat to A'ukre as a positive development:

Back in '91, when I made my final trip overseas ... I was already saying then that I wanted to stop traveling ... I was already thinking I had nothing more to say ... The other thing was that I wasn't taking anything back to my community. I don't want to speak any more to teach you [whites]. I returned with the assurance that I was bringing back something positive for my community. (interview with author Nov. 1995)

His self-assessment was tinged with a mixture of resentment and pride:

> Many people, including my Indian and non-Indian colleagues, think Payakan got burned, he's finished. No, I don't have to be invited by anybody to struggle. But when I see that nobody else wants to fight, I also don't want to fight. I don't own any Indians. I don't own the forest. I'm one of the people who have responsibility for the forest and nature. (interview with author Nov. 1995)

It is difficult to see how Payakan will carry out this self-proclaimed responsibility. He seemed to support recent initiatives to teach sustainable mining and logging techniques to the Kayapó:

> In the beginning, I had the idea that the Indian could learn how to extract gold. But neither NGOs nor the government gave this kind of help to the Kayapó. I tried to convince the Indians but I couldn't. But it so happened that the government managed to expel the miners with Kayapó support. Now is the time for the whites to teach the Indians how to manage certain techniques to extract gold without polluting or destroying the environment. (interview with author Nov. 1995)

But Payakan has not participated in these initiatives, nor in the establishment of Kayapó community associations. He seems marginalised, both in Kayapó society and in the white world. While his age-mates exercise leadership in village and town (one has become president of Redenção City Council), he seems to sulk.

It would be grossly premature to count Payakan out, however. In his early 40s, he is no longer a "young leader," but Kayapó culture still presents opportunities for him to exercise considerable influence, as Raoni has done. As time passes and the Kayapó face new challenges, they may need his formidable organisational skills and his audacity again.

I asked to take a picture of Payakan *en famille*, and he told me to come back at noon the next day. When I arrived with my camera, I was told he was not at home. Perhaps he did not want to pose as a smiling father or expose his children to the scrutiny of an uncomprehending world. Or perhaps he did not think it would do him any good. The first time I had seen him, at a Washington press conference in 1988, his features had been suffused with uncertainty and mistrust. No matter how far Payakan traveled, it seemed, the phantoms of 500 years of history still pursued him.

5

Yanomami Apocalypse

The news photograph looks as if it came from the Vietnam War: a strapping soldier in camouflage gear hoists a small, limp, almost naked body into the back of a cargo plane. But the caption says the picture comes from Brazil, not Vietnam. This frail human being is a Yanomami Indian, one of more than 1,500 who died under the assault of "civilisation" between 1987 and 1990. News of their fate led the American Anthropological Association to accuse the Brazilian government of complicity in genocide, and thousands of people around the world carried protest banners in front of Brazilian embassies. The international outcry pushed the Brazilian government to change its policies, demarcate a large area on its northern frontier for the Yanomami and provide millions of dollars' worth of medical care to the Indians.

Brazilian air force pilot carries Yanomami woman to
helicopter, Aemosh village, Roraima, 1990.
Photo by Charles Vincent/Instituto Socioambiental.

Yet, more than five years after the demarcation of their reserve, the Yanomami keep dying of malaria, sexually transmitted diseases, viral infections, river blindness and complications of malnutrition, among other maladies. Their traditional way of life is in ruins. The end of the world as they know it seems nigh. What has happened, what will happen, to the Yanomami, and why?

According to the Yanomami, the story began when Omamë, their creator, buried a lethal substance under the ground, from where its deadly smoke could not escape to poison them. "As long as the gold stays in the cold depths of the earth, everything's all right, it isn't dangerous," explains Yanomami leader Davi Kopenawa. From the sky and the forests come supernatural threats and diseases, but helper spirits controlled by shamans keep them at bay. Some of these helper spirits hold up the sky, so it will not collapse as it did once before, at the beginning of the world.

The Yanomami have lived in the forests of the northern Amazon for a very long time. Davi told anthropologist Bruce Albert (1991: 171): "Tell them how in the beginning ... how we were, how we had good health, how we weren't dying so much, we didn't have malaria. Tell how ... we hunted, how we held feasts, how happy we were."

The Ethnographic Present

Anthropologists who have studied the Yanomami since the mid-1950s tell different tales. Some recount constant conflicts between Yanomami villages, duels with clubs and machetes, ambushes in the forest, wife-beating, gang rapes and other forms of violence. Others say the communities they studied were not particularly violent. Ferguson's book claims that Yanomami warfare has correlated over hundreds of years with intrusions by outsiders and their goods, while other scholars call the Yanomami "the largest relatively isolated indigenous group in the Western hemisphere." The interpretation of Yanomami culture is still much contested.

Whatever the "true" picture, most observers agree upon a few facts. Because of the remote location of their territory and the geographic obstacles hindering contact, the Yanomami knew little of whites until missionaries began living among them in the 1950s. Scientists do not seem to have identified the Yanomami as one people until the 1960s (Ribeiro 1967, Galvão 1967). They have determined that the Yanomami speak four or five distinct languages that derive from the same linguistic trunk (Gomez 1997b).

Yanomami maintain extensive trading networks and alliances with neighboring villages, but their relations with more distant communities may turn hostile. They tend to identify themselves by village (populated by 40–300 individuals), rather than seeing themselves as part of the larger group, which numbers about 9,000 in Brazil and 12,000–13,000 in neighboring Venezuela. Nonetheless, their customs are similar across the large area in which they live. They believe that the forest around them teems with spirits – some helpful, some evil – which shamans can harness by going into trance under the influence of a hallucinogenic plant. When someone dies, the death is usually assumed to be caused by spirits mobilised by a hostile village. The Yanomami cremate their dead, pulverise their bones and mix the powder into a plantain beverage, which they reverently consume.

They live in large *shabonos*, round or oblong thatched shelters that house the whole village. Women gather forest plants and tend gardens, while men clear new gardens and hunt. Storytelling is a great art and a form of entertainment, as is political oratory. The Yanomami have a rich "oral literature." The shaman and the village headman are important figures, but neither can tell anybody what to do.

When the fertility of the gardens wanes, the supply of game decreases and tempers flare, Yanomami communities divide and groups go their separate ways, starting new villages and dispersing the population. They keep in touch via vast webs of trails through the forest, visiting other villages frequently. Spaces that look empty on the map "are in reality completely used by the Yanomami" (Distrito Sanitário Yanomami 1991: 14).

The problem with this description is that it is in the present tense, as if Yanomami culture had survived intact the deadly assaults of the past 30 years. Davi sadly observed, "We used to call the spirits to heal us. Today the Yanomami don't even build their big *malocas*, they just live in little huts in the forest, under plastic sheeting. They don't even plant gardens, they don't hunt any more, because they're sick all the time. That's how it is" (Albert 1991: 171).

It would be a mistake to see the Yanomami of 50 years ago as living in a timeless Eden (or a Hobbesian dystopia where life was nasty, brutish and short). For at least a hundred years, perhaps much longer, Ferguson says, the Yanomami have had access to machetes, cooking pots and other items from the outside world, via trading networks with other Yanomami villages and neighboring indigenous groups such as the Maiongong.

When whites began arriving in numbers in their territory in the 1950s, the Indians wanted their wonderful goods. A steel tool is many times more efficient than a stone axe. Visiting anthropologists and missionaries complained that the Yanomami would mercilessly importune them, only to give the objects away after a short time. "To be stingy is to be antisocial, to deny the inviolable reciprocity that governs relations between people. To breach such reciprocity was to trigger sorcery accusations, or bad feelings, to say the least," observed anthropologist Alcida Ramos (1995c: 8), who has studied the Sanumá sub-group of the Yanomami for more than 30 years.

Some missionaries would establish themselves in an area by giving away vast quantities of trade goods. Their attempts to convert the Yanomami to Christianity mostly failed. Sometimes they brought deadly contagious diseases, such as measles and tuberculosis, into the Yanomami world; but they have also provided life-saving medical treatment and education in the Portuguese language.

Anthropologists have also complicated the lives of the Yanomami. They arrived in Yanomami villages with stocks of gifts, and their presence inevitably affected the tenor of community life. Some may have inadvertently transmitted diseases and precipitated conflicts. According to Ferguson, there was little warfare among the Yanomami before anthropologists and other outsiders arrived, from the 1930s to the 1950s. When outsiders were present, however, rivalry for goods would increase and so would conflict. When they left, the constant flow of goods they had provided stopped, and villages went to war.

The Invasion of Civilisation

By that time, the outside world had intruded massively, in a far more destructive way. Large numbers of whites arrived in Yanomami territory in 1973, when the Brazilian government decided to build a highway across the northern Amazon. Construction crews brought contagious diseases such as influenza, measles and tuberculosis to Yanomami territory. Since the Indians had no immunity to these illnesses, many died. A perverse relationship of dependency and hostility, "mistrust and seduction," grew up between the Brazilian workers and the Indians (Medeiros 1995: 85).

In areas near the highway, Yanomami culture was devastated. Game fled, and the Indians begged for food instead of planting gardens. Pressure intensified on the Yanomami to abandon their traditional ways and assimilate into Brazilian society as the poorest of the poor. Yanomami living near the highway wanted Brazilian goods to prove that they, too, were "civilised," not "wild Indians" (Saffirio and Hames 1983: 19).

Ironically, only 250 kilometers of the proposed 1,500-kilometer highway were completed, 200 in Yanomami territory. Work was abandoned because of lack of funds in 1976. The Northern Perimetral Highway is a road to nowhere that brought disease, social degradation and conflict to the Indians (Ramos 1995c). It also brought Brazilians and other outsiders in ever greater numbers.

Along with freebooting prospectors, squatters, prostitutes and other poor refugees from the impoverished Northeastern region and Brazil's big cities came people of another sort: anthropologists, journalists, missionaries, physicians, young adventurers looking for a cause. In the early and mid-1970s several went to the Catrimani mission post, not far from the highway. Among them were John Saffirio, a Catholic missionary priest who became an anthropologist in order to understand the Yanomami better; Alcida Ramos and Kenneth Taylor, a Brazilian–British couple who passed through on their way to do anthropological research on the Sanumá; Bruce Albert, a French graduate student in anthropology; and Claudia Andujar, a Swiss photographer on a Guggenheim fellowship. Ramos, Taylor, Albert and Andujar became the nucleus of a group of outsiders who decided to dedicate themselves to defending the interests of the Yanomami.

In 1975 the Brazilian government conducted a satellite survey of Amazonian natural resources called RADAM, which found impressive deposits of gold, uranium, cassiterite (the basis of tin) and other strategic minerals in Yanomami territory. Also in 1975, Kenneth Taylor, then a professor at the University of Brasilia, drafted a plan to protect the health of the Indians who lived near the highway. It was never fully implemented, and "less than a year after it began, the project was cancelled due to the military's antipathy to a foreigner operating along the frontier" (Ramos 1992: 53).

Then the prospectors arrived. In 1976, 500 miners were deep in Yanomami territory, looking for cassiterite. The government expelled them after an international outcry at the dire results of their presence. The government also expelled Taylor, Ramos and Andujar, presumably because it did not want them monitoring exactly what was going on in Yanomami territory. The governor of

Roraima (then a federal territory) was quoted as saying, "An area as rich as this one can't afford the luxury of preserving a half-dozen Indian tribes and holding back development" (CEDI 1991: 164).

Claudia Andujar tried to return to Yanomami territory for three years. In 1978, she and some of the other "veterans" of Catrimani formed the Commission for the Creation of a Yanomami Park (CCPY). They presented to the federal government a project to demarcate a large reserve – about 7 million hectares. The military regime had its own idea about the proper dimensions of a Yanomami reserve. After the RADAM surveys showed where the minerals were, the military drew up a plan to create a number of "islands" where the Yanomami would live. Around them, prospectors would have free access to the mineral-rich areas. This scheme did not take into account the Yanomami's traditional way of life or the web of trading networks and trails that ramified throughout their territory. Indeed, it reduced the reserve's extent by 70 per cent. Also unaccounted for was the persistence of the prospectors, who, the government expected, would open up remote areas so that modern mining operations could move in afterwards.

More than 20 years later, the big mining companies have yet to establish themselves, while the garimpeiros keep invading Yanomami territory and the lands of other indigenous groups throughout the Amazon region.[1]

> The vast majority of these people were either underemployed or unemployed, smallholders who had lost their lands, or urban workers who had lost their jobs. Victims of the country's grossly unequal land and income distribution, these migratory human masses have been pushed off into Indian lands by the shock waves created by underdevelopment. (Ramos 1995c: 276)

Between 1970 and 1980, gold's international price increased 17 times. In late 1980, it reached $850 per ounce. In 1981, 2,000 miners invaded Yanomami territory to look for gold. Outbreaks of disease and violent conflicts between miners and Yanomami resulted. The Brazilian government's sporadic and feeble attempts to deal with the situation had little effect on the larger pattern, which has recurred again and again, from the mid-1970s to the present.

Parts of the Brazilian government worked against or contradicted the policies of other parts at various times. For example, in the mid-1980s FUNAI, the federal Indian protection agency, signed contracts allowing mining companies to explore for minerals in indigenous areas, including Yanomami territory. These agreements triggered garimpeiro invasions, epidemics, conflicts and other deadly consequences, so that the Federal Police, the army, the air force and other agencies had to go in and expel the miners. During certain government development projects, various federal agencies encouraged or even subsidised invasions of indigenous lands – by landless peasants, garimpeiros, loggers and others – that the federal courts eventually declared illegal. The same sad history keeps happening, with increasingly deadly results, as more Indians die with each invasion.

After 20 years, the Brazilian government cannot claim ignorance of the inevitable outcome of uncontrolled entry into Yanomami territory. Some observers wonder if the government has a more sinister goal, the Final Solution to the Yanomami Problem. Alcida Ramos bitterly called epidemics "efficient instruments for creating empty lands for white occupation" (Ramos 1995c: 275).

In 1983, anthropologists John Saffirio and Raymond Hames (1983: 19), both students of Napoleon Chagnon, commented, "As long as the Yanomami do not have full control over their aboriginal territory, from which their life derives, then they will not have the choice of staying as they are or becoming Brazilians."

The military had headed and controlled FUNAI, the Indian protection agency, since its founding in the mid-1960s, at the beginning of the military dictatorship. Anthropologists and indigenists deemed too sympathetic to Indians were periodically purged from the agency. But in 1984, as the 21-year dictatorship slowly approached its end, pro-Indian factions inside FUNAI asserted themselves by asking Claudia Andujar to advise them on Yanomami demarcation. Andujar had traveled throughout Yanomami territory in 1981 and knew its true extent better than anyone else. She stayed at the house of Alcida Ramos, recently returned to Brazil after several years' exile in Britain and still considered "suspect." Ramos wrote an anthropological justification for demarcating the largest possible area for the Yanomami: more than 9 million hectares (about 58,000 square miles) spanning Roraima and the state of Amazonas. No "islands," no mining areas. CCPY's proposal became the official basis for demarcating Yanomami territory.

Demarcation is a rather tortuous, time-consuming and polemical process requiring field research, geographic surveys and a series of legal procedures that usually take years. Once accomplished, demarcation guarantees indigenous people "preferential use and control" of the land they live on, but the land remains the property of the federal government. According to Brazil's 1988 Constitution, Congress is supposed to determine subsoil rights on a case-by-case basis. Before 1988, various federal agencies could sign mining and logging agreements with private companies "on behalf of" indigenous groups. Despite a Constitutional provision mandating demarcation of all indigenous territories by 1993, only 238 of Brazil's 566 indigenous areas had been completely demarcated by the end of 1995 (Instituto Socioambiental 1997). Chronically underfunded, FUNAI never seems to have sufficient resources to carry out this or other responsibilities.

In February 1985 a ragtag gang of 40–60 garimpeiros led by José Altino Machado, a mining entrepreneur, invaded Yanomami territory, besieging the FUNAI post at Surucucus for five days. Machado wanted to mine cassiterite in the area, but FUNAI had signed an exclusive contract with a big mining company. The Federal Police finally expelled and arrested Machado and his "troops." The significance of this event went unremarked at the time, but it came at a crucial moment: the end of the military dictatorship and the beginning of an indirectly elected civilian government. Machado would keep appearing – in Yanomami territory, in Brasilia at Congressional hearings, even at the 1992 Earth Summit in Rio de Janeiro – as the Roraima garimpeiros' principal spokesman.

In 1986, before the military's Calha Norte project became public, the Brazilian air force enlarged an airstrip at Paapiu, in the heart of Yanomami territory. "Declaring the strip to be a national security area, they had the Indian communal house within it destroyed and went away" (Ramos 1995c: 276). Ramos believes this action was in preparation for Calha Norte colonisation efforts. The Paapiu airstrip would soon become the main entryway for tens of thousands of invaders.

In the wake of the Calha Norte leak, the military launched a public relations campaign to defend their development plans for the Amazon. Reviving the national security ideology that they had used to legitimate military rule, they claimed in interviews and articles that Calha Norte was necessary to defend Brazilian sovereignty from an alleged conspiracy to "internationalise" the Amazon. The Yanomami and other indigenous groups living near the border were pawns of "ultra-leftists," multinational corporations, Catholic bishops, the CIA and others who wanted the Amazon's riches for themselves. These "outside agitators" were encouraging the Yanomami to set up an independent state straddling the Brazilian–Venezuelan border. Foreign forces were just waiting for an opportunity to sweep across the border. Demarcation of a Yanomami reserve was, therefore, a threat to national security. To neutralise this threat, the military said it needed to set up military posts all along the northern frontier and "Brazilianise" the region by encouraging colonisation of its "empty spaces" by "civilised" people.

Nonetheless, Senator Severo Gomes of São Paulo state publicly proposed the formation of a 9-million-hectare Yanomami Park, which would cover 36 per cent of Roraima's territory. Gomes became an important ally in the Yanomami's struggle for survival.

As the military disseminated its vision of Amazon development and candidates campaigned to participate in the Convention that would draft Brazil's eighth Constitution, something ominous was happening in Roraima. In May 1987 Davi Kopenawa sent a letter to President Sarney, alerting him to a massive garimpeiro invasion of Yanomami lands. A month later Sarney replied that he was aware of the problem and the government was working on it.

The following account, which summarises the tortured history of the Roraima gold rush of 1987–90, was compiled by CEDI (Ecumenical Information and Documentation Center 1991: 172–93), a Brazilian non-governmental organization.[2] It shows how genocide happened with the complicity of the Brazilian government, and how international pressure helped end it. Most of the information comes from Brazilian press reports.

Anatomy of a Genocide

In June 1987, Federal Police prohibit food shipments to garimpeiros inside Yanomami territory, but the Garimpeiros' Association obtains an injunction permitting the shipments.

In August, four Yanomami are killed in a conflict with garimpeiros near Paapiu. Garimpeiros plant a news story saying eight garimpeiros were killed; the Federal Police investigate and say the report is false. FUNAI requests that Federal Police forcibly expel all anthropologists, missionaries and medical personnel from Yanomami territory. Federal Police carry out the expulsions.

Claiming that the armed forces and Roraima business interests support them, in September the garimpeiros refuse to leave Yanomami territory. By December about 2,500 garimpeiros are working in Yanomami territory. A month later, an estimated 10,000 garimpeiros are extracting 30 kilograms of gold daily in Yanomami territory.

After news of the gold rush reaches the outside world, 197 Italian parliamentarians call for emergency aid for the Yanomami in February 1988. Six Brazilian senators (including future President Fernando Henrique Cardoso) denounce the genocide of the Yanomami in an April letter to President Sarney. The United Nations Environment Program informs the Brazilian government that it has awarded the Global 500 Prize to Yanomami activist Davi Kopenawa. The Brazilian government does not release this information until August.

By August, one Indian per day is dying of malaria or disease resulting from contaminated water in Roraima, but FUNAI President Romero Jucá says most Yanomami deaths are due to old age, not disease.

The next month FUNAI proposes a Yanomami reserve divided into 19 "islands," reversing its earlier support for a 9.4-million-hectare reserve. President Sarney names Romero Jucá governor of the newly created state of Roraima. Indians denounce to the Attorney General 20 Yanomami deaths due to mercury poisoning and disease.

In October 1988 Survival International organises weekly demonstrations at 20 Brazilian embassies around the world to protest the 19-island demarcation plan. These demonstrations will continue for more than three years. Nonetheless, Governor Jucá states his support for the garimpeiros and proposes that medical supplies and food be distributed to them. Ex- (and future) Governor of Amazonas Gilberto Mestrinho invests in a mining project inside Yanomami territory.

A federal judge orders that three missionaries be permitted to return to Catrimani mission in November. Within a month, FUNAI asks for a judicial order forbidding the missionaries' return.

In February 1989 the United Nations Secretary General receives a petition with 250,000 signatures protesting the genocide of the Yanomami. President Sarney ratifies the 19-island plan. He then signs decrees creating two national forests in Yanomami territory. "Entry or residence by third parties or the exercise of any activity without prior authorization of FUNAI and IBAMA (the environmental protection agency) is prohibited," the decree declares (cited in CEDI 1991: 172–93).

In April the Venezuelan National Guard expels Brazilian garimpeiros found 100 kilometers inside Venezuelan territory. On April 19, the national Day of the Indian, General Bayma Denys, the head of the National Security Council, declares that expelling garimpeiros from Yanomami territory is "impossible." Later that day, he promises Davi Kopenawa and another indigenous activist that the army and the Federal Police will expel the garimpeiros.

A VIP delegation headed by Senator Severo Gomes visits Yanomami territory in June. Meanwhile, Governor Jucá proposes garimpeiro "reserves," road paving and other development projects in Yanomami territory, to facilitate mineral exports. By July, 50,000 garimpeiros are estimated to be working in Yanomami territory. At Boa Vista airport, 400 light aircraft going to and from mining areas are making up to 15,000 landings and take-offs daily. The VIP delegation publishes a report, "Roraima: Warning of Death," and calls for repeal of the 19-island demarcation plan. The federal Attorney General's office brings a suit in the federal court to close illegal airstrips and expel garimpeiros from Yanomami lands. Mining entrepreneur José Altino Machado visits the Ministry of Mines and Energy with three Yanomami, who say nothing.

Kayapó leader Raoni visits the Minister of the Interior in August and asks that garimpeiros be expelled from Yanomami lands. Two other indigenous activists visit Nagasaki, Japan, and ask the Japanese government to cut off aid to Brazil until the garimpeiros are expelled. President Sarney personally promises Raoni that the garimpeiros will be expelled. Garimpeiros kill two Yanomami near a Calha Norte barracks.

Garimpeiros claim in September that Paranapanema, one of Brazil's biggest mining companies, is trying to have them expelled from Surucucus, so that it can begin mining cassiterite there. Demanding the garimpeiros' expulsion, leaders from eight indigenous groups try to see President Sarney, who does not receive them. They dance around the statue of Justice near the Presidential Palace. The Presidential Guard surrounds the Palace to keep the Indians away. Sarney later says he did not know the Indians were there.

In October, Governor Jucá says he has signed an agreement with the National Department of Mineral Research, transferring responsibility for mining to the Roraima state government. This seems to be illegal under Brazil's new Constitution. A federal judge orders the closing of 9 million hectares of Yanomami territory to outsiders and the expulsion of all garimpeiros in the area. IBAMA, the environmental protection agency, announces that it is studying the establishment of small "industrial units" for timber and mineral exploration in the Roraima National Forest, inside Yanomami territory. FUNAI says it has no resources to expel garimpeiros; state and federal security forces will have to do it.

Garimpeiros attack Yanomami in November, killing three to five; Yanomami wound three garimpeiros in retaliation. Garimpeiros close a nearby airstrip so that Federal Police and FUNAI cannot investigate. Elton Rohnelt, owner of Gold Amazon mining company, future Congress member and "a businessman who has accumulated a fortune estimated at $20 million during 15 years in the jungle" (CEDI 1991: 186), says he wants to help the Yanomami. "We invaded Indian lands, so we're obligated to preserve them and find a way for them to live," he says. His idea is "to integrate the Indian into the community through work."

More than 120 Yanomami are in the Indian House in Boa Vista, Roraima, and another 200 are in various hospitals, suffering from malaria. Two weeks later, 214 Indians with malaria are at the Indian House. FUNAI's regional office reports that between January and August, 59 died. FUNAI medical teams are flying the sick out of Yanomami territory in air force helicopters.

As the Yanomami death toll rises in December, a federal judge orders the air force to close illegal airstrips in Yanomami territory. Congress appropriates funds for emergency medical aid to the Yanomami. President Sarney signs a decree expelling the garimpeiros within 90 days and setting up a medical assistance program. On 15 November, Fernando Collor de Mello is elected President of Brazil with 52 per cent of the vote. His inauguration is scheduled for 15 March 1990.

In January 1990, Federal Police and FUNAI report that 82 illegal airstrips are serving 200 mining sites in Yanomami territory. Three-fourths of the gold mined in Roraima is smuggled to Venezuela and Guyana. Federal Police prevent small planes from using Boa Vista airport. Around 400 garimpeiros demonstrate in protest, blaming the Bishop of Roraima for the shutdown. Romeo Tuma, director-general of the Federal Police, arrives in Boa Vista to command the expulsion operation. After meeting secretly with garimpeiro leaders, he agrees to the establishment of garimpeiro "reserves" inside Yanomami territory. Justice Minister Saulo Ramos supports the agreement, saying, "No judicial decision can determine the impossible."

The Attorney General's Office threatens to issue arrest warrants for the president of FUNAI, the director-general of the Federal Police and the air force minister if they don't carry out the expulsion. Nonetheless, the expulsion operation ends after two days, leaving most of the garimpeiros inside the Yanomami area. Tuma denies having agreed to the garimpeiro "reserves." A flurry of announcements, decrees, injunctions and counter-orders follows.

At the end of January, the Justice Minister takes full responsibility for implementing the expulsion order.

After visiting Paapiu in February, the Justice Minister says he saw Yanomami children so malnourished they "looked like Biafrans." He then issues an arrest warrant for French photographers who took pictures of a Yanomami child dying of malaria, which led to an international outcry. The photographers are charged with "failing to give first aid."

Prince Charles gives a speech in which he criticises the Brazilian government for its treatment of the Yanomami. President Sarney decrees two garimpeiro "reserves" inside Yanomami territory. The Justice Minister says the reserves have been created to prevent the miners from spreading diseases to other parts of the country. The Attorney General issues a bill of impeachment against the President, for flouting the garimpeiro expulsion order.

Sarney leaves office in March with impeachment charges pending. A week after his inauguration, President Collor visits Yanomami territory and orders the dynamiting of 110 illegal airstrips. The new governor of Roraima, a Collor appointee, says, "We can't stand with our arms crossed, eyeing a mountain of gold." Severo Gomes visits the new Justice Minister, Bernardo Cabral, and asks for enforcement of the expulsion order and repeal of the 19-island demarcation plan and the garimpeiro "reserves." The order expelling the missionaries from Catrimani is overturned in federal court. In April, President Collor calls for "further study" of Yanomami reserve boundaries.

The next month, a Roraima judge issues orders permitting mining and airstrips in Yanomami territory. FUNAI's regional coordinator in Roraima says in June that dynamiting the airstrips is ineffective, because the garimpeiros quickly rebuild them. A constant stream of Yanomami arrives in Boa Vista for emergency medical treatment. Davi Kopenawa is laid off from his job as a FUNAI interpreter.

The VIP Delegation publishes a report in July, saying the situation of the Yanomami has not improved. Dynamiting the airstrips was, in its judgment, "just a show." Around 5,000 garimpeiros remain in Yanomami territory. The rivers are contaminated by mercury, and the fish population has plummeted; hunting is poor. At least 1,000 Yanomami have died in two years. In August the Foreign Minister informs the Justice Minister that the international community views Brazil as "an agent of genocide."

In September garimpeiros attack a Yanomami village, killing two and wounding one; two garimpeiros are also killed. The Attorney

General asks for a federal genocide investigation in this case. The President of FUNAI sends a demarcation order, repealing the 19-island plan and establishing a 9.4-million-hectare Yanomami reserve, to President Collor in October. He signs it.

At the end of 1990 the Justice Ministry runs out of funds for the expulsion operation on 17 December. Garimpeiros are said to be on their way back to Yanomami territory.

After the Genocide

About 15 per cent of the Yanomami in Brazil may have died during the three-year gold rush. In Surucucus and Paapiu, the centers of garimpeiro activity, 65 per cent of the indigenous population was infected with malaria, most with the deadly falciparum strain. Before the garimpeiro invasion, malaria had been rare; afterwards, it became endemic. Among the Yanomami 35 per cent were malnourished, and 76 per cent were anemic; 13 per cent of children lost one or both of their parents. Some of the orphans were sent to Brazilian households in Boa Vista, where they probably became domestic servants. This dispersion, plus the abandonment of villages where mortality was high, devastated Yanomami culture and disaggregated Yanomami society in many areas. "In the last 15 years, the Yanomami have gone from being an exotic and fierce people to becoming a symbol of indigenous peoples on the verge of extinction" (Ramos 1995c: 281).

The difference between this process and previous decimations of indigenous groups is the extent of its documentation. Despite the remoteness of the region, the Yanomami died in plain view, and each excruciating step along the path to genocide was recorded. Millions of people around the world watched. Many protested. Everyone involved in trying to save the Yanomami seems to agree that international outcry and pressure did make a positive difference. But the international public has a short attention span. More horrible human catastrophes soon replaced the Yanomami as subjects of international concern.

The terrible effects of the gold rush did not end, even when most of the garimpeiros left Yanomami territory (usually for other indigenous areas). In March 1991 Alcida Ramos visited the Sanumá for the first time in many years and found the group in a pitiable state. Although the Sanumá lived far from the centers of garimpeiro activity, malaria had spread to their region and 71 per cent of the population was infected. One of the side-effects of malaria is anemia. The visiting medical team "instead of getting a drop of red blood for the microscope slide, drew a diluted pinkish liquid" (Ramos 1995c: 295).

Everywhere Ramos went, people were ill. Entire communities had dispersed, not because their members had died, but because they did not have the strength to collect or store food. Ramos made a difficult and dangerous journey to Boa Vista, over "countless rapids and waterfalls," because the Brazilian air force helicopter usually available for such trips was "out of service." She could not find a doctor to return to the Sanumá with her, only a "health attendant." Back in Yanomami territory with three colleagues, a week's walk from Surucucus, she heard that the air force had suddenly withdrawn its support for the Yanomami health program; there would be no more helicopters. "We were stranded in the middle of nowhere for more than ten days, during which I had ample opportunity to be infected by malaria," whose effects she felt after she returned home.

As the military withdrew from the health program, garimpeiros began entering Yanomami lands. Ramos and her colleagues had no idea who would find them first. Finally the National Health Foundation (FNS), the federal agency sponsoring the program, hired a small helicopter to take them to Surucucus. Five people and 180 kilograms of equipment made a frightening half-hour trip in the overloaded helicopter. Ramos was furious at the capricious attitude of the FNS and the military.

> It is one thing to be aware of the global and irrevocable process of Western domination that engulfs all indigenous peoples. It is another thing to observe the sordid details of the here and now – the cynicism, the murder or the neglect – that go into the making of this domination. (Ramos 1995c: 312)

The International Response

Early in 1991 the American Anthropological Association (AAA) sent Terence Turner to Brazil to investigate the situation of the Yanomami. He was the chairman of a special AAA commission whose members included Alcida Ramos and Bruce Albert; Claudia Andujar and Davi Kopenawa were consultants. The commission's report lambasted the Brazilian government for its "attempts ... to avoid its responsibilities to protect the welfare, lands, resources and social integration of its indigenous nations" (American Anthropological Association 1991: 1). In considerable detail, the report documented the government's sins of omission and commission and the devastating effects of the gold rush on the Indians' health and culture. Yanomami territory had become "a death camp for its own people," the commission charged.

Turner published an op-ed piece based on the report in *The New York Times* during President Collor's state visit to the US in June 1991. At the same time, commission member Steve Schwartzman, of the Environmental Defense Fund, persuaded eight US Senators to send a letter to the Brazilian government expressing their concern about the Yanomami. The AAA also sent the commission's report to international non-governmental organisations, scientific associations, the Inter-American Human Rights Commission and multilateral funding institutions such as the World Bank. These actions triggered critical US media coverage of Brazil. At about this time, anthropologist Gale Goodwin Gomez, who studies Yanomami linguistics, sent information about their situation to the UN Human Rights Office. UN Secretary General Perez de Cuellar then expressed his concern about the Yanomami in a private chat with Collor. The day after his return home, Collor fired the president of FUNAI and named a new commission, more likely to favor the Yanomami, to restudy reserve boundaries.

This is a classic example of the power of international pressure, strategically applied.

Demarcation and After

President Collor announced the demarcation of a 9.4-million-hectare Yanomami reserve on 15 November 1991, one of Brazil's most important national holidays. Many seemed to think that the Yanomami's problems had been resolved. Few garimpeiros remained in the area at the time; but by mid-1992, when the Earth Summit convened in Rio de Janeiro, some 11,000 garimpeiros were said to be working in the reserve. The expulsion operation was reactivated, and by September 1993 only 600 remained, most in Venezuela.

At the 1992 Earth Summit in Rio de Janeiro, Collor gloried in his new reputation as a protector of indigenous peoples. As a result of the demarcation and several environmental initiatives by his government, Brazil won promises of more than a billion dollars in loans and other international aid. But six months later Collor was out of office, the first President of any country in the Americas to be successfully impeached, for corruption. Collor maintained his ousting had been a coup by retrograde elements of Brazilian society, threatened by his "modernising" measures. His Vice-President, Itamar Franco, became President in January 1993. Franco was notable for his erratic, unpredictable behavior and his nationalistic prickliness.

CCPY published disturbing reports throughout 1993 of epidemics and conflicts between Yanomami and garimpeiros. But the world's attention seemed to be elsewhere until mid-1993, when three spectacular incidents of savage violence highlighted the deep crisis of Brazilian society. On 23 July 1993, eight street-children were killed in front of the Candelária Church in downtown Rio de Janeiro. About a month later, on 29 August, hooded police invaded the slum of Vigário Geral, on the outskirts of Rio, in the middle of the night and randomly killed 21 unarmed men, women and children, some while they slept. In between, news came of the massacre of 16 Yanomami men, women and children by garimpeiros. Though announced in mid-August, it probably happened in June and July, in two stages. Because of the remoteness of the location, it took weeks for the news to reach Brazil's capital. Gale Goodwin Gomez, who was doing research in Yanomami territory at the time, faxed a message about the massacre to the UN Human Rights Office in New York.

The Justice Minister announced the Yanomami killings on nationwide television and then went to the reserve to investigate, an indication that the Brazilian government took the incident very seriously. So nervous was the government about international repercussions that the Foreign Ministry denied a Canadian and a US diplomat access to the area, despite the Justice Minister's invitation.

During the following days, the estimated number of victims kept rising, from 16 to 40 to 73, to possibly more than 100; it seemed as if the Justice Minister and the President of FUNAI were competing to give the most horrific accounting. Meanwhile, the head of the Federal Police, whose responsibility is to investigate crimes committed in indigenous reserves, publicly expressed doubts that a massacre had happened. There was, he insisted, no direct physical evidence – no bodies, only a few burnt bone fragments – and a burnt-out village. Yanomami cremation rituals leave almost no traces; afterwards, they never mention the names of the dead again.

Politicians from Roraima and other Amazon states echoed the police chief's skepticism. The Army read satellite signals to determine exactly where the massacre had occurred, and discovered that it had happened just inside Venezuelan territory. The story faded into the back pages of Brazil's and the world's newspapers.

About two weeks after the Justice Minister's announcement, Brazil's biggest television network reported what seemed like an authoritative version of events. Reporters and cameramen followed Bruce Albert across Roraima to the neighboring state of Amazonas. There he met with a group of Yanomami who had fled the scene of the massacre about a month earlier and walked almost 200 kilometers through the jungle. As the cameras rolled, Albert called names from an official list of presumed victims. One after another, 60-some Yanomami refugees raised their hands, indicating that they were very much alive (Albert 1993).

Story of the Massacre

After interviewing the survivors, Albert published a long and harrowing article detailing the terrible events of June and July that had culminated in the massacre at Haximu. Though it had occurred in Venezuela, there was no doubt that Brazilian miners had planned and carried it out. The motive was escalating tension between the miners and Yanomami villagers who were dependent on them for food and goods.

"The Indians turn from being a threat to being an annoyance with their incessant demands for the goods that they are accustomed to receiving ... If gifts and promises do not get rid of them, then the solution is to intimidate or even exterminate them" (Albert 1996: 203). According to testimony gathered from Indian and Brazilian witnesses, 15 garimpeiros, four ringleaders and four hired gunmen set out to kill all the inhabitants of two malocas, some 85 people, in a series of attacks.

Most of the victims died at Haximu. "After a few very long minutes, the miners stop shooting and enter the shelters in order to finish off anyone still living. Machete blows kill not only the injured but also the few who had not been hit; they mutilate and dismember the bodies that are already riddled with buckshot and bullets" (Albert 1996: 206). This attack caused the deaths of four adults and eight children or adolescents.

The survivors "will never forget that the whites are capable of cutting up women and children, just like 'people-eating spirits.'" They consider the garimpeiros inhuman, "not even fit to be enemies" (Albert 1996: 206).

While fleeing to the other end of Yanomami territory, the Indians quickly conducted the customary funeral rituals. "The belongings of the dead have to be disposed of, the personal names obliterated, and their ashes either buried or ingested" until all traces are gone. Otherwise, the ghosts of the dead would "wander between two worlds, haunting the living with interminable melancholy even worse than death" (Albert 1996: 206).

Thus the Indians destroyed most of the material evidence of what had been done to them. But according to Aurelio Rios, the Assistant Attorney General for Indigenous Affairs, enough remained at the crime scenes to show that the massacre had really occurred. Some 20 garimpeiros were arrested in the weeks following the massacre; all but two, thought to be the ring-leaders, were quickly released. "But once media attention turned elsewhere, a local judge quietly released them [and] the two immediately disappeared ..." (Brooke 1995b: 1). A federal prose-cutor told *The New York Times* in 1995 that seven suspects (the only ones whose full names were known) might be tried in absentia for the massacre in 1996. At the end of 1996, the federal court delivered a precedent-setting verdict of genocide against five defendants, all of whom were still at large. If this case follows the pattern of other indigenous massacres, those responsible will never be punished.

The Nationalist Reaction

Opponents of indigenous rights claimed that the massacre was the invention of the international press, the Catholic Church or the NGOs that supported Yanomami demarcation. The Governor of Roraima called the killings a "pseudo-massacre" and equated the Yanomami's funeral ritual with cannibalism. True to his nation-alist principles, President Franco commented, "It's not whether people died or not that matters, but the fact that we have to keep an eye on Amazonia" (CCPY 1993 *Update*).

For the Brazilian government, "keeping an eye on Amazonia" meant pushing through a project that the military had long advo-cated: installation of a sophisticated radar surveillance system that would cover the entire region. The armed forces also proposed that they be given additional funding to revive the moribund Calha Norte program, intended to "Brazilianise" the frontier with military outposts and agricultural settlements.

Another result of the furore over the massacre was the creation of a new "Amazon Ministry," with Rubens Ricúpero, then Brazilian ambassador to the US, at its head. By mid-September 1993, Ricúpero had taken over the Environmental Secretariat as well, to create a new Ministry of the Environment and the Amazon.

The military's reaction to the massacre was ominously complacent. The commander of the Jungle Infantry Brigade, João Paulo Saboya Burnier, was quoted in August (Martins 1993):

> The Yanomami tribes should, in our opinion, be acculturated gradually, with respect to their characteristics. They should be oriented to emerge from indigence ... Without a doubt, this will take away the Indians' cultural identity, as happened with your ancestors and mine ... The danger isn't the occurrence of a confrontation between Indians and Brazilian citizens.

The army minister, General Zenildo de Lucena, said in an interview (Cubel 1993) after the massacre:

> Who knows if the Yanomami, after they're acculturated – on the frontier with Venezuela and with relatives on the other side – who knows what they'll want later on? This is a half-crazy idea, but we have to worry about it. There is no Yanomami nation. They're tribes. We can't keep them isolated from the world ... We'd have a zoo if we kept these Indians for research in the future. We can't leave the Indians without the benefits of civilisation. I believe it has to be something progressive, done scientifically ... One solution is the humanisation of points on the frontier ... It would be a kind of colonisation.

Clearly, the military had not surrendered its determination to decide the development of the Amazon region – and if that meant the disappearance of the Yanomami as a people, so be it.

Aligned with the military were members of the Amazon bloc in Congress, who kept introducing bills to repeal the Yanomami demarcation or drastically reduce the size of the reserve. These efforts continued for years, although FUNAI's new President, Márcio Santilli, insisted in late 1995 that the demarcation was a fait accompli.

Elton Rohnelt, the fabulously wealthy mine owner, federal deputy from Roraima and assistant leader of the government party in the Chamber of Deputies, led the forces against Yanomami demarcation. In an interview with the author in November 1995, he said:

> I know the Yanomami, because I lived with them. They don't travel much. They're not healthy, they're weak, they can't walk far. They don't have proteins, they're not protected. They die at age 30, 33 at the most. Their biochemical make-up has no protection. Their diet is horrible. Their lives are short. What's most important – to protect their culture? They don't have a culture, they're primitive Indians, they have sub-cultures that they acquire from other tribes. They don't have a rich culture, they're poor in culture – either let them end their lives at 30 or 35, or try to help them attain [civilisation]. Are we whites being selfish, when in the First World we try to lengthen our life spans, spending millions of dollars – aren't we being selfish when we let them live to 35, because we want to keep them the way they are?
>
> This is a hypocrisy on the part of the world, those who don't know about the problem – the NGOs especially. Of the NGOs in Brazil, if 5 per cent are serious, that's a lot; 95 per cent are there to get money from abroad and set up campaigns, invent stories, to get dollars from abroad.
>
> The hypocrisy is in the world's wanting the Yanomami to stay the way they are, with no help from FUNAI, which doesn't have resources, with no other form of assistance, letting them die of hunger and malaria. There are some international health organisations there trying to work, but that isn't enough ...
>
> We don't want the Yanomami area transformed into a zoo-logical garden of men and animals. We want the Yanomami in a reserve with legitimate, good assistance, so they can survive.
>
> I don't see any action by the NGOs, the Brazilian government, FUNAI or anybody to solve the problem of the Yanomami, who keep on dying.

The problem, he continued, is that too much land was given to them, it should be decreased. "Talk, talk, talk doesn't resolve anything." Here his tone became harsh.

When asked for his suggestions, he snorted slightly and said:

> Revise the criteria for demarcation, everything's included in that: all the necessary studies to re-study the Yanomami problem and see if it's important to have 9 million hectares or not ... For example, I think all the Yanomami should stay on the Pico da

Neblina [Brazil's highest mountain], in upper Amazonas, a place where there's much more game and it's already a National Park. They should stay there rather than in Roraima. I don't see why they should stay in Roraima. In Roraima there's no game for them, nothing.

The fact that the Yanomami have lived in Roraima since time immemorial and have first rights to their territory according to the Brazilian Constitution apparently means nothing to Rohnelt and his allies. Their rhetoric provides the backing for continuing attacks on the Yanomami and other indigenous groups who get in the way of Brazilian economic and military activities in the Amazon region.

"Genocide by Omission"

The massacre of 1993 was one incident among dozens of killings of Indians in Roraima since the mid-1980s. The only difference between it and the others was its magnitude. Many more Yanomami have died of contact diseases spread by miners than in violent confrontations with them. As long as garimpeiros continue to enter Yanomami territory, the Indians will suffer the consequences of their presence. Thousands still come in every year. At the end of 1995, for example, the Federal Police and FUNAI announced yet another multimillion-dollar operation to remove 4,000 garimpeiros from Yanomami lands. The operation did not take place until late 1997, and its results were meager.

Even when garimpeiros are no longer present, the diseases they brought in have remained or even spread to more remote areas. Despite an elaborate and expensive government–NGO health program, the number of disease victims continues to grow. According to the National Health Foundation, the government agency that coordinates the Yanomami health program, 25 per cent of Brazil's Yanomami population has died since 1987. Deaths increased by 34 per cent from 1995 to 1996 (CIMI 1997e).

Unlike some other indigenous groups in Brazil, the Yanomami are small, delicately built, with a physique that belies their reputation for internecine violence and feuding. To outside invaders, they look vulnerable. Few have guns or ammunition and so are easy targets for armed garimpeiros. Entire villages languish in the grip of malaria, tuberculosis, river blindness and other vicious diseases. Their ability to defend themselves against unscrupulous and violent intruders is thus severely limited by illness, hunger, and lack of weapons or protection.

Unfortunately for the Yanomami, they live scattered across international boundaries. Thus they have become pawns in a political struggle, between the Brazilian military and its civilian opponents, to define "national security." The military and their allies in Congress and the private sector play the same nationalist card every time the Yanomami become the objects of international concern. A British journalist summarised the nationalist argument soon after the reserve was demarcated:

> It's all the fault of the Catholic Church, whose priests, agents of foreign powers, are secretly stacking up vast troves of gold and diamonds. It's all the fault of the multinationals, who want to encourage an independent Yanomami nation which they can go into and rape of its minerals without trouble.
>
> It's all the fault of the CIA, which wants to destabilise Brazil to stop it joining the ranks of the superpowers. It's all the fault of foreign bankers who want to stop Brazil exploiting its mineral riches to keep the noose of debt around the country's neck.
>
> Such are the views expressed publicly not by a crackpot minority but by senior politicians, generals and business leaders. (Pisani 1991)

This orchestrated response to international expressions of humanitarian concern – plus indigenous people's geographic and psychological remoteness from most Brazilians, racist sentiments and unacknowledged guilt – dampens public sympathy for the Yanomami. This translates into a general lack of political support in Brazilian society for the protection of indigenous rights or demarcated territories. Diffusely anti-indigenous rhetoric dominates public discourse on these questions, and defenders of indigenous groups must struggle to be heard. With the exception of Davi Kopenawa, no Yanomami speak for themselves on television or in newspapers; they appear only as anonymous, voiceless victims.

How Can the Yanomami Defend Themselves?

The Yanomami define themselves as members of villages, allied with or against other villages, rather than as members of a single people or nation. Claudia Andujar estimates 200-some Yanomami villages in Brazil, spread across a vast territory, divided by four or five different languages. Consequently they have not yet managed to unite against the overwhelming external forces threatening their survival. Few Yanomami speak or understand Portuguese, and only a handful have acquired schooling. Those that do, such as Davi Kopenawa, learned Portuguese at mission schools, usually in villages located near highways or Brazilian settlements. Villages in remote areas have little opportunity to come to grips with the outside world. The number of potential leaders capable of dealing with, or even understanding, Brazilian society is very small.

In 1983, Saffirio and Hames noted (1983: 5), "The major stumbling block they have in making ... decisions is their gross ignorance of the long-term consequences of whatever decision they do make." Twelve years later, Rohnelt commented, "The poor things don't even know what's happening to them" (interview with author Nov. 1995).

At the request of local Yanomami leaders, CCPY has begun work on a pilot project to establish village schools. Teaching the Yanomami how to defend themselves against the assaults of civilisation is an urgent task. Training future leaders will be a long-term undertaking. It remains to be seen if CCPY, anthropologists, doctors, missionaries and others who have already devoted decades to helping the Yanomami will have sufficient time to succeed in these efforts. Brazilian anthropologist Marco Lazarin, who has studied the Yanomami for several years, admits, "I'm very afraid of what's going to happen to the Yanomami ... whether they're going to survive as an indigenous group or not" (interview with author Sept. 1995).

With the encouragement of neighboring indigenous groups, who have been in contact longer with Brazilian society and know better how to cope with it, the Yanomami have begun to respond more assertively to the outside world. Early in 1996, more than 280 Yanomami leaders, representing 27 villages, met for four days at the Catrimani River in the "Third Assembly of the Yanomami People," to discuss their situation and make alliances with neighboring indigenous groups and organisations.

They issued a "Letter to the Chiefs of the Whites" – the President of Brazil, the Justice Minister, the President of FUNAI and the Attorney General. In the tone of a ceremonial oration, the letter said:

> We Yanomami meet here in great friendship. After making this great alliance, we commit ourselves to the defense of our land.

We ourselves write this letter, because we think it important to send our words to the chiefs of the whites.

We don't want garimpeiros on our land, because they are very bad: they pollute our rivers and creeks; they make holes in our land searching for gold; the game die, the fish die, the crayfish die, along with the crabs and alligators. All the fish die. All the Yanomami are dying because the garimpeiros bring diseases that kill us: they bring malaria and influenza. For this reason we don't want garimpeiros or other whites: ranchers, politicians, loggers, soldiers, fishers ...

We don't want a small territory. We want a large area, the way it was demarcated. Don't reduce the size of our land. We want to keep this large, unbroken area.

That's what we Yanomami leaders think.

Fernando Henrique Cardoso, President of Brazil, Nelson Jobim, Justice Minister: even though you are both chiefs, you allowed yourselves to be scared by certain whites; you became afraid ...

We Yanomami, after strengthening our alliance with the Macuxi of CIR, are ready to confront the whites in defense of our land. (CIMI 1996a)

The Yanomami will need as many allies as they can muster in their coming confrontations with "the whites." Continuing international pressure, assistance from Brazilian groups, indigenous mobilisation on the regional, national and international levels, infusions of financial aid – all will be necessary. In the past, outside attention has waxed and waned, according to the vagaries of news gatherers. The Yanomami need constant allies – people willing to help them confront long-term issues such as education, medical care, political organisation and sustainable economic development. Without this kind of coordinated, ongoing work, the Yanomami may disappear, as have hundreds of other indigenous groups during 500 years of Brazilian history.

The next challenges facing the Yanomami are even graver than seasonal invasions of garimpeiros and outbreaks of killing diseases. In 1995 the Brazilian and Venezuelan governments announced that they had signed agreements to jointly develop their frontier regions. According to a Venezuelan NGO, plans include paving a road from the Brazilian border all the way to Caracas, installing electrical lines to transmit power from a Venezuelan dam to Boa Vista, and, most ambitious of all, linking the Amazon and Orinoco Rivers via a canal. In every case where similar development projects have been carried out, indigenous peoples have suffered catastrophically.[3]

Davi Kopenawa warns (Albert 1991: 170):

Not only the Yanomami will die – all of us will die together. When the smoke fills the breast of the sky, it will also die, just like the Yanomami ... The sky will be torn apart. The Yanomami shamans who have died are many, and they will want to take revenge ... they'll want to cut the sky into pieces so that it will collapse on top of the earth. They'll also make the sun fall, and when it falls, everything will become dark. When the stars and the moon fall, the sky will be dark. We want to tell all this to the whites, but they don't listen ...

6

Davi

A recent documentary film about the Yanomami, *Warriors of the Amazon* (CSL Films 1996), stirred fascination and sympathy, revulsion and shame in many viewers. In some scenes the Indians seemed beautiful and fragile, threatened human beings whose vulnerability cried out for help. In others, they seemed as frighteningly unpredictable and menacing as members of an unknown species. They were the Ultimate Other: mysterious, unknowable, remote.

I was reminded of Napoleon Chagnon's books and films, which had done so much to influence, if not determine, my views of the Yanomami. Like thousands of other college students, I first read *The Fierce People* at the impressionable age of 19 or 20. Years later, many of its descriptions of Yanomami violence still seemed repulsive, as much for Chagnon's gusto in the telling as for the violence itself:

> One of the young men took the wife of another because she was allegedly being mistreated by the husband. This resulted in a brutal club fight that involved almost every man in the village ... When the husband's rival speared his opponent, the headman went into a rage and speared him in turn, running his own sharpened club completely through the young man's body. He died when they tried to remove the weapon. The wife was then given back to her legitimate husband, who punished her by cutting both her ears off with his machete. (Chagnon 1983: 172–3)

Anthropology students (and some of their instructors) still cringe at one of Chagnon's films, about Yanomami drug taking. They watch green mucus pouring from the nostrils of Yanomami warriors dancing and chanting under the influence of a hallucinogenic powder. All the scholarly explanations (and the sight of Chagnon himself, befeathered and painted, prancing about in a drug-induced trance) cannot eclipse that image.

Davi Yanomami at the United Nations.
Photo by Claudia Andujar, Comissão Pró-Yanomami

Jacques Lizot's austere, scrupulous accounts of Yanomami daily life, stripped of explanation, also do not seem to show Yanomami culture in a positive light. Other anthropologists avoid the problems created by Chagnon's emphasis on violence by writing drily abstract analyses. It is their personal stories of their fieldwork experiences that stir empathetic responses in the reader.

Yet some of the anthropologists who studied the Yanomami have fallen in love with them. Photographer Claudia Andujar took thousands of pictures of their delicate beauty and then dedicated her life to trying to save them from extinction. Was this devotion the mere obverse of revulsion? Or had Andujar and the anthropologists attained a higher level of understanding by spending years in the forest with the Yanomami?

The rainforest is a magical place; perhaps its enchantment created an aura around the slight, painted, combative bodies of the Yanomami for those who visited them. But for many Northerners, Chagnon's portrayal seems indelible.

In *Warriors of the Amazon*, when Yanomami talk to the camera, they seem like anyone else: people with motives, explanations, rationales. But when they visit the former enemy village – rushing in, shaking bunches of 6-foot-long arrows, hurling bloodcurdling cries like spears, pantomiming assault on their hosts, who sit silent, unmoving, on the ground – they seem so startlingly strange as to be incomprehensible.

In an early scene in the film, a visiting shaman undertakes a cure. Finding the sickness he once sent to torment his enemy in his enemy's knee, he sucks it out with gusto. He jumps up and spits a silvery thread of mucus into his hand, then holds up the dripping trophy. In a recent interview, Chagnon remarks, "Real Indians get dirty, smell bad, take hallucinogens, belch after they eat, covet and sometimes steal their neighbors' wives and make war. They're normal human beings" (Alcântara 1995: 7). If the Yanomami were just like us, however, Chagnon would have had few readers. Their radical differentness challenges our definitions not only of normality but of humanness. Anthropology students are assigned to read about the Yanomami to prod them into rethinking those definitions.

While Northerners thousands of miles away create idealised images of indigenous people, Brazilians on the frontier have no scruples about expressing frankly derogatory views of Indians. After the Haximu massacre, the governor of Roraima snorted, "In truth, what the Indians do is cook the limbs of the body and eat them like bananas" (Brooke 1993b: A4). This was his description of the Yanomami funeral ritual, in which they cremate the dead, pulverise their bones and mix them into a plantain gruel, which they reverently drink.

A foreign journalist noted, "The term 'Indian' is used as a term of abuse in Brazil. It implies dirty, lazy, ignorant." The Bishop of Roraima commented, "Brazil has always wanted to dominate and integrate the Indian, to denigrate, to humiliate" (Pisani 1991: 26).

People far from Brazil and its 500-year history are more likely to think of the Yanomami as threatened and vulnerable human beings. Horrified by the terrible stories about Yanomami genocide in the 1980s, thousands protested in front of Brazilian consulates and embassies around the world for years. They welcomed Davi Yanomami to their countries and thrilled to his eloquent, apocalyptic prophecies.

The Ambassador

Davi has many faces. He seems innocent and sophisticated, profound and simple, tormented and serene. After the Yanomami massacre of 1993 he painted his face black and danced a war dance. A photograph shows him holding arrows, looking over his shoulder at the camera, radiating unvarnished hatred, as if he were thinking: "You white bastards, you killed my people, why should I say another word to you, ever?"

Another Davi, calm ambassador from the Fourth World to the First, weaves eloquent words for audiences across the world. Then he goes home to share the fate of his people. As a shaman, he is respected as a leader by the Yanomami. Seeking nothing for himself, he goes to the outside world and returns with goods for all. He lives as everyone else does in the village.

It is almost too easy to present Davi as an avatar of virtue. In a bitter essay called "The Hyperreal Indian," anthropologist Alcida Ramos, who has done much to help the Yanomami, says whites insist on putting Indians into a noble straitjacket. The acceptable Indian hero, she says, is "dependent, suffering, a victim of the system, innocent of bourgeois evils, honorable in his actions and intentions, and preferably exotic" (Ramos 1994: 163). But Davi is something more than this: a leader and man of action, as well as a poet and prophet.

Davi's quiet concentration, dignity and firmness make him an attractive personality. He bears no apparent resemblance to Chagnon's picture of the fierce Yanomami. Each time I meet him,

I feel that in any culture, he would be considered a good man. It is hard to say what this goodness consists of, but it is a recognisable quality, almost an aura. Davi presents a comprehensible, sympathetic image of the Yanomami to the world.

Davi has much greater success outside Brazil, where he is an exotic visitor and prophetic visionary, than inside the country, where he is just another Indian, an obstacle to "progress." In Brazil (and many other places) Indians are not seen as persons. During 500 years of competing with Indians for land and resources, Brazilians have shown undisguised, sometimes murderous, contempt for them. Davi, however, has managed to move through the looking glass of culture and become something other than the Other.

He is a short, stocky but not heavy man with a broad, placid face. His habitual expression is serious, attentive. Claudia Andujar, who may know him better than any other white person except Bruce Albert, says he is "very clever, very independent, very curious" (interview with author Oct. 1995). She first met him in the mid-1970s, when he was in his twenties, working for FUNAI, the federal Indian protection agency, as an interpreter. He was one of a handful of bilingual Yanomami.

They met in a village where, as a result of road construction, 50 per cent of the population had died. When she heard about the village, Andujar, who was working as a nurse's aide at Catrimani mission, sent a message to FUNAI, asking for emergency help. FUNAI took a month to send assistance. In the meantime, she and her companions decided to walk (a five-day journey) to the village. They stayed, doing what little they could, until a FUNAI helicopter arrived; among the passengers was Davi, working as an interpreter. Years later, when they met again, Davi reminded her of their first encounter. He had never forgotten her effort to help his people. "Then somehow we started to work together ... we became friends" (interview with author Oct. 1995).

The End of Isolation

Davi was born in 1955 in an isolated village in the Toototobi region of Yanomami territory. As a child he learned to read the Bible in Portuguese from New Tribes fundamentalist missionaries. He left the village in 1967, after his mother died of measles brought in, Bruce Albert says, by the missionaries.

As Claudia Andujar tells the story:

The New Tribes [Mission] wanted to make out of him a pastor. That's how he started to learn how to read and write.

Then he got very sick, he had to be taken to Manaus. He had tuberculosis. Then he had his first contact with the city and was invited to work with FUNAI. So he had already various influences. Somehow in all these groups, people must have felt that he had a very good head, no? and tried to attract him to become a leader or an important person, but in a partisan way.

I know that at a certain point he wasn't sure if he should become an evangelical pastor or not. And then suddenly he turned against it. He decided that what they were doing was something that didn't go along with his upbringing ...

Then he went and worked with FUNAI ... Suddenly he saw the penetration of the road builders and his people getting sick ... Through the indigenist movement he met other indigenous leaders who were fighting for a similar cause, and this identified him with the problems of his own people. Afterwards he definitely was an engaged person, who started to fight for his people in a global way. (interview with author Oct. 1995)

In the late 1970s Davi worked at Demini as an interpreter for FUNAI. There he married the daughter of a village leader and shaman, who taught him the rudiments of religious practice. Appointed head of the FUNAI post, he became a liaison between the Yanomami and the Brazilians, a distributor of trade goods and a political leader, with no conflict, Bruce Albert says, between his traditional and modern roles. Albert calls him an "intercultural mediator par excellence" (interview with author March 1997).

Andujar and other activists working with Brazil's indigenous movement needed spokespeople to make the issues real to international audiences. People like Davi were – and are – rare. He has witnessed his people's decimation and can communicate its enormity to people worlds away. More than that, he has the capacity to enlist their support. For these skills he won the United Nations Global 500 Award in 1989.

Others with similar talents and backgrounds, like Paulinho Payakan, have been damaged or brought down by their international prominence. "We never wanted him to be a VIP," Andujar says of Davi. She maintains he has remained unaffected by his experiences in the North. Andujar is partly responsible for this, it seems. An ageless, statuesque woman with an evocative alto voice, she sometimes travels with him. "He often says I'm very strict. We have a very curious relationship, we joke together, we respect each other" (interview with author Oct. 1995). She attributes the success of their working relationship to his personality and his understanding of the need to abide by the rules of the outside world as long as he is in it.

According to Bruce Albert, Davi experienced a tumultuous childhood and much emotional turmoil. For a while he wanted to be white but could not manage it. Under the influence of his father-in-law, an important shaman, he became calmer and more self-confident. His wife insisted that the family live in her village, not at the FUNAI post where Davi was in charge. Their children are fully integrated into village life.

At home, Davi is an activist as well as a visionary. He wants bilingual education – reading, writing and counting – for Yanomami children, even as they continue to live in traditional ways. Providing teachers and educational materials to more than 200 villages spread over 9.4 million hectares is a daunting task. It is one of the main priorities of CCPY, but finding the funds and personnel has been difficult.

In June 1996, CCPY reported that after nine months of work, 33 Yanomami in Davi's village had learned to write words, sentences and paragraphs in their mother tongue, and 12 were reading syllables. Meanwhile, however, many Yanomami children do not live long enough to go to school. Despite a federal health program that maintains 23 outposts, Yanomami infant mortality rates due to malaria, dehydration, upper-respiratory infections and other diseases remain frighteningly high. In 1995, 62 per cent of Yanomami deaths were among children under five (Magalhães 1995: 2); 20 per cent of Yanomami infants die before their first birthday.

The Organiser

In 1993 Davi tried to turn a dream into reality by supervising the construction of an airstrip inside Yanomami territory for health care teams to use (Zacquini 1993). First he traveled the world seeking financial support for his project. Back in the village, he rounded up Indians to do the work and paid them with trade goods. Soon, half of the people working on the strip or living by it had contracted malaria.

Instead of hunting and gathering in the vicinity of the strip, the workers walked 40 minutes to four hours to obtain food provided by CCPY, which slowed the work considerably. When neighboring

Yanomami came to visit the construction site, tools went missing. (Metal tools are prime trading goods that travel along networks stretching for hundreds of miles throughout Yanomami territory.) Davi kept bringing presents to the workers, but they were "never enough."

Carlo Zacquini, a priest who has worked for many years with the Yanomami, reported:

> Toto did not come back in January for the second round of work, as he had promised earlier. The reason he gave was always the same: the need to organise and to take part in festivities. One of these, in Novo Demini, ended in a fight and, as a result, most of the men were unable to work for several weeks. (Zacquini 1993: 2)

For the Yanomami men, feasts were important political and social events that demanded their presence and took priority over Davi's project.

Then an ant invasion, probably caused by the human invaders' disturbance of their habitat, made work difficult and drove the medical team out of their hut.

At first Davi had insisted that the Yanomami could do the work of building the airstrip themselves. Eventually work stopped completely, and Davi had to ask CCPY for help. The Indians did build a clinic, but Davi did not accomplish all he had dreamt of. Given the difficulties of life in the rainforest, his capacity to conceive and coordinate such a project is impressive enough.

Davi is most effective as a defender of his people. Perhaps influenced by his early training in evangelical Christianity, he has developed a powerful mythological discourse that synthesises Western and Yanomami concepts to express the fears and beliefs of both Yanomami and Northern audiences. He speaks "to defend the forest and keep my people from disappearing." He told Albert he came to understand his duty in a shamanic trance, when he had a vision of the forest being destroyed.

Davi finds the Northern idea of "preserving" or "protecting" bits of "nature" ridiculous, however. "What you whites call 'the environment' is what remains of what you destroyed" (Albert 1995: 20). He recognises that some whites, like Chico Mendes, are enlightened enough to be educable in Yanomami teachings, and he feels his mission is to overcome white ignorance. In his "Letter to All the Peoples of the Earth" (Yanomami 1989), he concluded, "I, Davi Yanomami, want to help the whites learn with us to make the world a better place."

The Prophet

To this end, Davi carefully translates Yanomami concepts into Portuguese terms acceptable and comprehensible to Northern audiences. But he believes whites are deaf and blind to the spiritual meaning of his words. He told Albert that whites think they are so intelligent because they mistake words for reality. It is the Yanomami who understand the true nature of reality.

The Yanomami traditionally viewed other peoples, and especially whites, as "subhumans, peripheral and unintelligible" (Albert 1995: 5). They still regard whites as little better than cannibals, because they kill Yanomami children. In Davi's mythological vision, the principal evil spirit, Xawara, embodied in smoke and pollution, is:

> ... white, and all the details of his macabre expeditions are linked to his whiteness: he has hired guns to capture his victims, he cuts their throats with a machete, he skins them to make hammocks, he fries them in big ovens, he throws their entrails to his hunting dogs, he grills their bodies and keeps them in wooden boxes or vacuum-sealed cans. (Albert 1995: 14–15)

Xawara "kills and eats our children ... he's hungry for human meat" (Albert 1995: 15). Mercury fumes from the gold extraction process are the form of Xawara that the Yanomami know and fear. But smoke (from forest burning and industrial pollution) contaminates not only the forest but the world beyond, even threatening the sky and, thus, the equilibrium of all life on earth.

> As long as the gold stays in the cold depths of the earth, everything's all right, it isn't dangerous. When the whites take the gold out of the ground, they burn it, they put it on the fire as if it were flour. This makes smoke come out of it. That's how the Xawara that is gold smoke is created. Then this "smoke epidemic" spreads through the forest, where the Yanomami live, but also through the land of the whites, everywhere ... When this smoke arrives at the breast of the sky, the sky begins to get very sick, it also is affected by Xawara. The land gets sick, too ... There's also smoke from the factories. You think that God can drive away this smoke, but he can't. He too will end up dying, even though he's a supernatural being ... (Albert 1995: 16)

For Davi it is imperative to protect not only the forest but the shamans and their traditional knowledge. They are the ones who mobilise the guardian spirits that keep the heavens from falling down. But "the Creator has already left this world and gone far away and will not create any more Yanomami." And without the Yanomami, the earth is doomed.

At the opening ceremony of the International Year of Indigenous Peoples at the United Nations in December 1992, Davi told the General Assembly:

> The leaders of the rich, industrialised world think that they are the owners of the world. But the shamans are the ones who have true knowledge. They are the real first world. And if their knowledge is destroyed, then the white people too will die. It will be the end of the world. This is what we want to avoid. (Brazil Network Jan.–March 1993: 6–7)

Like any prophet, he has no hesitation about "speaking truth to power."

As time passes and Yanomami continue to die of contagious diseases or in violent confrontations with invaders, Davi's vision becomes more vividly threatening:

> We try to put an end to the Xawara, but it's very resistant. It's wrinkled and elastic, like rubber. The spirits can't cut it with their weapons, and it grabs them when they attack it.
>
> The whites don't think, "The sky will collapse," they don't say to themselves, "The Xawara is devouring us." So she's[1] eating a bunch of children, she does away with them, eats them without stopping, kills them and grills them as if they were monkeys that she'd hunted. She piles up a bunch of grilled children ... Xawara is very hungry for human meat, doesn't want to hunt fish, only Yanomami meat ... When the smoke fills the breast of the sky, it will also die, just like the Yanomami. When it gets sick, continuous thunder will be heard. The thunder will get sick and it will bellow in anger without stopping, as a result of the heat. The sky will be torn apart. [The spirits will] cut the sky into pieces, so that it will collapse on top of the earth. They'll also make the sun fall, and when it falls, everything will become dark. When the stars and the moon fall, the sky will be dark. (Albert 1991: 71)[2]

Western depictions of similar intensity can be found in the fresco of Hell in the Baptistery of Florence Cathedral, or in Revelation:

> And he opened the bottomless pit; and there arose a smoke out of the pit, as the smoke of a great furnace; and the sun and the air were darkened by reason of the smoke of the pit. (9:2)

> ... and there fell a great star from heaven, burning as it were a lamp, and it fell upon the third part of the rivers, and upon the fountains of waters ... (8:10)

> ... and the third part of the sun was smitten, and the third part of the moon, and the third part of the stars; so as the third part of them was darkened, and the day shone not for a third part of it, and the night likewise. (8:12)

Davi's apocalyptic vision is no literary conceit, however; it expresses his realistic fears for the future of his people.

> If the garimpeiros keep going through our forest, if they don't go back home, the Yanomami will die, they'll really be finished. There won't be anybody left to cure us. The whites that cure us, doctors and nurses, are few ... Only a small number of us will survive. Many people have already died, and I don't want to let everybody else die. (Albert 1991: 71)

In a desperate race against time, disease and neglect, Davi has harnessed the eloquent oral and religious traditions of the Yanomami to their sense of natural superiority and made a powerful, poetic vehicle out of his prophecies. He has traveled around the world on it, but he always returns to the village to share the Yanomami's life and fate. On his journeys he has acquired a unique breadth of knowledge:

> I also see white people suffering in the city, hunger, everything expensive, homelessness, lack of food, everyone is suffering. ... Our custom is better than that of the whites, because we preserve the rivers, floodplains, lakes, mountains, the hunting, the fish, the fruits
> ... The mining activity taking place on our lands is not only illegal, it is also harmful to the miners themselves. Many of them are held like slaves. Like us, they also are victims of the greed of the handful of men who control the gold trade. (Yanomami 1989: 68)

Davi is the only Yanomami who has managed to gain the attention of the outside world. Few others have learned enough Portuguese to communicate with Brazilians; there is no educational system in the reserve, aside from the occasional missionary school, a long-running educational project at Catrimani and CCPY's recent literacy project.[3] Most Yanomami still have only indirect contact with outsiders. Some of the adult Yanomami who have learned Portuguese over the past generation have thrown in their lot with the prospectors and loggers who seek to extract their territory's natural riches.

Davi is trying to pass along his knowledge of the outside world and his sense of mission to other Yanomami, and he takes them along on his trips whenever possible. Even with the help of sympathetic and devoted outsiders like Claudia Andujar and Bruce Albert, however, Davi's lonely crusade may not be sufficient to save his people. An anthropologist in the reserve in late 1996 reported that Brazilian miners and soldiers were giving guns and ammunition to Yanomami men, who were using them to kill one another.

The director of the federal government's Yanomami health program commented:

> Traditionally the Yanomami have diverse levels of friendship or antagonism in relation to the population groups with whom they have direct or indirect contact. Normally the antagonism is resolved in arguments within the family, confrontational rituals such as blows to the thorax or duels with wooden posts, or raids by warriors. Deaths rarely result from these confrontations ... The introduction of firearms has altered the situation drastically. Small disputes may end in shooting when people lose their temper ... The inherent lethality of firearms provokes extreme situations. (Magalhães 1996: 3)

He observed that as tensions rise, people hide in remote areas and stop going to health posts to seek medical attention. Consequently, overall death rates rise. "It alarms me to think that this problem could become chronic" (1996: 4), he concluded.

It seems inescapable: to survive physically and culturally, the Yanomami must stop expending their energies on internal conflict, redefine themselves as one people and unite to defend their lives and lands from outside impingement.

The "Third Assembly of the Yanomami People", in January 1996, was a step in that direction. Davi's name was first on the list of leaders, and the words in the meeting's final declaration sounded like his own. With CCPY's help, he played a central role in organising and leading the meeting. But his commitment to education comes from his recognition that his leadership alone is not enough. A new generation of leaders, conversant with the outside world, must continue the task of mobilising the Yanomami. Education takes years, however, and the Yanomami are struggling with urgent problems – epidemic malaria, river blindness, childhood diseases, invasions – that may destroy them before a new generation of leaders can emerge. Unless he oversees a miracle, Davi Yanomami may be remembered as a lonely, tragic figure whose words were lost in the smoke of Xawara.

7

Fit for What?

It is all too easy to predict the end of an indigenous group. Experts have been doing so for hundreds of years, and they have often been wrong. As a result of the systematic, massive depredation of the world's tropical rainforests during the past 40 years, however, it is not unreasonable to fear the end of the indigenous peoples who live in them.[1] Hundreds of indigenous groups have already disappeared, and many more struggle to maintain their traditional ways of life against tremendous odds. They live with disease, hunger, violence and poverty, not only in Brazil but in Indonesia, Siberia, Australia, the United States and many other countries. Destroy their means of subsistence, and what (or who) can stop them from vanishing completely?

Ticuna family in 1993, near the site of the 1988 massacre.
Photo by Linda Rabben.

Governments, multilateral lenders, multinational corporations, private banks and other institutions may not be counting on the convenient disappearance of indigenous peoples who get in the way of their ambitious development plans, but they often act as if they are. In April 1997, the presidents of Brazil and Venezuela ceremonially inaugurated a road building project to connect Caracas with Manaus. The road threatens the wellbeing of at least eight indigenous groups and the environments from which they draw their sustenance (InterPress Service 1997a). The following month, the Pemon Indians of southern Venezuela forced workers to stop constructing high-tension power-line towers across a national park where they live. According to an Internet report from the EnviroNews Service (Hamilton 1997), "The action came as a result of the state-owned company CVG-EDELCA and INPARQUES [the Venezuelan Parks Institute] failing to reply to letters from the Pemon pleading for information and consultation." By law, the authorities were required to respond to affected communities within 15 days.

Also in May, 20 Venezuelan environmental groups protested the federal government's "gross abuse of power and deceitful manipulation of public opinion" in granting mining concessions in a forest reserve in the same region, where the Pemon and several other indigenous groups live (Centeno 1997). The Indians and environmentalists said these projects contravened federal laws protecting forest reserves, national parks and indigenous rights. In both cases, the government failed to notify or consult those affected by its plans.

After months of public controversy, in October 1997 the Venezuelan government announced it would not grant any more concessions in the Imataca forest reserve until the Supreme Court decided on the constitutionality of the decree authorising them. The Supreme Court then pronounced the decree authorising the concessions unconstitutional, but the environment minister announced that the decision did not apply to him. The issue remained unresolved at the end of 1997 (AMIGRANSA 1997).

Under years of unremitting pressure from grassroots groups and non-governmental organisations, governments and the giant institutions that dominate the world's economic life have created international agreements, regulatory regimes, laws and policies to protect vulnerable environments and people. Yet they continue to plan and carry out mega-projects that may lead to the destruction of those fragile communities and their environments.

A recent report from Amazon Watch (Soltani and Osborne 1997) analyzed eleven giant development projects proposed or in progress in seven Amazon countries: highways, dams, oil and natural-gas pipelines, electric power lines, industrial waterways and railroads with construction costs in the billions of dollars. Most will facilitate production and export of minerals, agricultural commodities and timber to world markets, but are unlikely to improve the lives of these countries' poor majorities, who lack balanced diets, adequate sanitation, clean water, health care, decent housing, sufficient wages to feed their families and basic education. Multinational corporations, capital investors, national elites and Northern consumers will be the main beneficiaries. The immediate and long-term environmental and social costs of devastating large areas and numerous communities to build these projects have not been fully calculated.

Publicly funded institutions like the World Bank may have changed their method of participation in such projects, but not their development model. "The private sector now accounts for more than 75 percent of project financing in the developing world while the MDBs [multilateral development banks] play the role of mobilisers of capital [rather] than that of direct lenders," notes the Amazon Watch report (Soltani and Osborne 1997: 7). The MDBs have spurred privatisation programs that decentralise the process of development funding. Consequently, the report warns, "Pressuring MDBs and governments is no longer sufficient to stopping destructive projects." Since loans now go to unaccountable corporations instead of governments, "disclosure and community consultation policies do not apply," and "these institutions do not adhere to the hard-won environmental and social lending policies of the traditional MDBs" (Soltani and Osborne 1997: 7).

Like the Kaingang Indians who attacked telegraph workers in the 1920s, indigenous groups have tended to confront the shadowy forces of international development on the ground, where they experience the projects' direct effects. In February 1997, for example, the Krikati of Maranhão, on the eastern edge of the Brazilian Amazon, set fire to two electric-transmission towers. Fed up with invasions of their territory, whose demarcation they have sought for 30 years, they waited with bows and arrows for the police. Two days later, the Xokleng of Santa Catarina state, in southeastern Brazil, invaded a dam site and opened four sluices, threatening to flood cities downstream. They were demanding indemnification for 856 hectares of flooded land (CIMI 1997a). These actions forced the federal and state governments to pay attention to the Indians' grievances, but there was no guarantee the problems would be resolved once the spotlight was turned off. In recent decades, the pattern has been for the government to respond under pressure with promises of immediate corrective action, after which nothing has happened. In the 1980s the Kayapó and other groups took to videotaping their meetings with authorities, so they would have evidence of government commitments to use in court proceedings or public confrontations.

The Kayapó Method

The Krikati and Xokleng may have been following the Kayapó's example. For almost 20 years, the Kayapó have been staging spectacular actions against government officials and others who tried to enter or take their land without their permission. Each time, the outsiders backed down, if only for the moment. In "going international," by mobilising Sting, visiting world capitals and influencing global public opinion, the Kayapó have shown other indigenous groups that such tactics can also work.

Over time the Kayapó changed their strategies for gaining the material benefits of "civilisation" without abandoning the traditional ways they valued or destroying the environment that sustained them. For many years they raided their neighbors, but this was an inefficient means of obtaining the goods they wanted. Later, when selling off resources to outsiders brought adverse consequences, they expelled miners and loggers from their territory. This action did not usher in an era of sustainable development, however.

The Kayapó are still struggling to earn sufficient money to buy the goods they want, provide education in Portuguese for their children and health care for all community members. Two communities formed associations to create and manage development plans, but as of mid-1997 they had not obtained funding. Anthropologist Terence Turner was advising a Kayapó gold mining project that showed some promise as a source of community income (personal communication 1997). Some villages were trying to develop eco-tourism or sustainable extraction projects. At the same time, however, loggers were making deals with some Kayapó leaders to cross their land on the way to extract timber illegally in another reserve. In late 1996, pressure from state politicians and private interests prevented the demarcation of a sizable part of traditional Kayapó territory called Baú. Then word came that the Brazilian government was again seeking funding, this time from private investors, for the Xingu dam project the Kayapó had stopped in 1989 (Melloni 1997). Tu'ire, the young woman who placed her machete on the side of the Brazilian bureaucrat's face at the 1989 Altamira meeting, told Turner in mid-1997 that she was ready to take up her weapon again.

For the Kayapó and other indigenous groups, the challenges and dangers of "integrating" into Brazilian society while preserving their culture will not end. The Indians need to prepare themselves for repeated confrontations and crises. This means having adequate resources (and a social structure) to mobilise leaders and participants. Readiness also requires cultivating allies in the outside world. The Kayapó have succeeded in doing all these things – indeed, they seem to have an aptitude for coordinated political action. They have operated independently, which may work for them but not for others.

Groups with fewer resources, like the Krikati and Xokleng and others, have sought help from the Missionary Indigenist Council, the Instituto Socioambiental and other non-Indian allies, but they may also need to join forces with other indigenous groups and create regional political blocs. To give a recent example of such collaboration, in mid-1997 the Tupinikim and the neighboring Guarani of Espírito Santo, Brazil, sent representatives to Europe to urge investors there to sell their stock in a multinational cellulose company that was challenging their demarcation rights under Decree 1775/96 (World Rainforest Movement 1997).

In November 1997, Guyanese indigenous groups joined to issue a statement declaring:

> We believe that we have the right to participate in decisions about the use of our lands and to give our consent prior to any form of permission being granted to logging, mining and other companies operating on or near our lands. Instead of granting mining concessions on our ancestral lands, we demand that the Government fully recognize our rights to these lands in accordance with international law ... we the Touchaus [chiefs] and Councilors have formed the Region 9 Amerindian Council to fight against the granting of these concessions and to represent us on other pressing issues.

The Indians complained:

Recently, persons contracted by the Government to demarcate our lands arrived unannounced in our communities. In light of the refusal of the Government to address all outstanding Amerindian land issues, we the Touchaus, village Councilors and other community leaders of Region 9 hereby declare that all work on demarcation of our lands cease immediately until such time that there be:

i) proper consultation and communication with all village councils and Amerindian communities;

ii) that these communities mentioned in (i) above, demarcate the land that they consider theirs;

iii) that the Government recognize and certify the areas demarcated by these communities.

Finally, they passed the following resolution:

Whereas past and present administrations have not addressed Amerindian issues in a satisfactory manner;

Whereas instead of having true consultation we have had autocratic decision-making by the Government on Amerindian issues;

Whereas the Minister of Amerindian Affairs is not representing Amerindian interests;

And, whereas it is time for us the Amerindians to organize ourselves for our own development;

Be it resolved that the 1st Conference of Region 9 Touchaus and other community leaders unanimously agree to form a Region 9 Amerindian Council to coordinate and manage our own development in cooperation with the Government and other sympathetic organizations and to work in solidarity with other Amerindians in this country for our own mutual benefit. (Amerindian Peoples Association 1997)

It is clear from the language of rights, international law and self-determination in these resolutions that the Indians have learned much from their contacts with international advocacy organisations. And it seems likely that they will increasingly form inter-tribal coalitions, councils and other collaborative structures to increase their political and economic power regionally, nationally and internationally. Such complex organisational efforts will require much time, energy and human – as well as financial – resources.

The Yanomami's Dilemmas

The Yanomami have only recently begun to unite to defend themselves. The perils facing them are formidable:

- epidemic diseases that kill potential leaders, weaken the population and disaggregate society,
- inadequate medical and educational assistance,
- geographic remoteness that impedes communication (it took six weeks for news of the 1993 massacre to reach the outside world, and another three to four weeks to determine the number of victims and whereabouts of survivors),
- lack of protection against armed invaders,
- lack of political leadership and support – allies are too few and too far away,
- no effective control over economic resources.

The Yanomami are fortunate in having Brazilian and international supporters who have devoted themselves to the Indians' welfare, who are managing to obtain financial support for development efforts, and who encourage them to organise. It is uncertain, however, if the Yanomami can pull together to fight the next series of battles, against the new generation of bilateral mega-projects that threaten their existence as a people.

The Bases for Caring

Why should we care about what happens to the Yanomami and the other indigenous groups that struggle to survive civilisation? What difference would it make if they disappeared? Aside from sentimental and humanitarian reasons for supporting indigenous people, there are strong political, environmental and scientific reasons for defending their cause.

After hundreds of years of destroying peoples who got in their way, the world powers contemplated Auschwitz and recoiled, if only temporarily, from their death-dealing arrogance. Fifty years ago they wrote the Universal Declaration of Human Rights, which established the foundation of a new political order, based on the rule of law and respect for all human beings. It is worth reviewing the first three paragraphs of the Universal Declaration's Preamble:

Whereas recognition of the inherent dignity and of the equal and inalienable rights of all members of the human family is the foundation of freedom, justice and peace in the world,

Whereas disregard and contempt for human rights have resulted in barbarous acts which have outraged the conscience of mankind, and the advent of a world in which human beings shall enjoy freedom of speech and belief and freedom from fear and want has been proclaimed as the highest aspiration of the common people,

Whereas it is essential, if man is not to be compelled to have recourse, as a last resort, to rebellion against tyranny and oppression, that human rights should be protected by the rule of law ... (Center for the Study of Human Rights 1992: 6)

Article 3 of the Universal Declaration declares, "Everyone has the right to life, liberty and security of person." Other articles outlaw slavery, torture, arbitrary arrest and detention, and guarantee equal protection before the law. Most of the world's nations have signed and ratified this document, which has become the foundation of international human rights law.

The noble sentiments of the Universal Declaration and the International Covenants of civil, political, economic, social and cultural rights have not been realised, but they do provide the bases for actions to protect and defend basic human rights around the world. Indigenous people have the same human rights as other human beings. Additional agreements, such as International Labor Organization Conventions 109 and 169, guarantee indigenous groups' rights to live on their traditional lands and follow their traditional customs.[2] Governments have committed themselves to protecting those rights, both through international treaties and in their national laws.

When a multinational oil company signs a concessionary contract with a government and then takes over part of an indigenous community's land without adequate consultation or compensation, it and the government may be violating international and national law. This fact in itself makes nothing happen. The United Nations sends no troops, the Inter-American Human Rights Commission makes no protest, the US government does not break diplomatic relations with the country, and the International Chamber of Commerce does not criticise the company's action. In one such case (which unfolded in 1996–7), the U'Wa indigenous community of Colombia repeatedly posted messages on the Internet, with the help of international environmental and indigenous-support organisations. The U'Wa threatened collective suicide if the corporation did not respect their decision not to allow oil exploration on their land. Internet users sent letters to Colombian officials, the company, the European Parliament and US Congress members, calling for action to protect the U'Wa's human rights. Similar cases happened in 1996 and 1997 in Ecuador, Brazil, Guyana, Venezuela and Surinam. By pressuring governments, international institutions and private companies in these ways, indigenous people, allied with citizens of many countries, were seeking to implement principles enunciated in international law.

In a statement to the World Bank/International Monetary Fund annual meeting in September 1997, Amnesty International pointed out that "development is all too often being pursued at the expense of human rights" and urged the multilateral financial institutions "to take civil and political rights as seriously as economic and social rights, and recognize the indivisibility of all human rights" (Amnesty International 1997).

Like other indigenous groups, Brazil's indigenous peoples have basic human rights, guaranteed in international agreements and the nation's Constitution, which uphold their control over their traditional territories and their entitlement to the same services and protection the Brazilian government is legally obligated to provide to all its citizens.

Economic Rationales for Protecting Indigenous Peoples

For those who do not consider moral and legal reasons for supporting indigenous peoples sufficiently compelling, ecologists have calculated the monetary value of what used to be called "externalities," environmental costs associated with large-scale exploitation and consumption of natural resources often found on or in indigenous lands. At the 1997 meeting of the American Association for the Advancement of Science, Stanford University ecologist Gretchen Daily pointed out that "goods and services" provided by natural ecosystems – including purification of air and water, recycling of wastes, generation and maintenance of soil fertility, pollination and foods – are worth trillions of dollars. "Humanity came into being after most of these services had been in operation for hundreds of millions to billions of years. They are so fundamental as to make them both easy to take for granted and hard to imagine disrupting beyond repair, as human activity threatens to do today."

Although Daily admitted that "it would be absurd to try to estimate the value of natural processes in strictly economic terms," she wanted decision makers to be aware of nature's incalculable importance for all societies (Environmental News Service 1997).

Do Indians Save the Environment?

Traditionally, Indians exploited the forest without destroying it. Some anthropologists and biologists believe that their shifting cultivation methods over the centuries have preserved and even enlarged the forests. Recent satellite pictures show that Brazilian indigenous reserves have the most undisturbed forests in the Amazon.

Environmental justifications for defending indigenous rights are not always clearcut, however. Increasingly, Indians are not left to their own devices. Once in contact with outsiders, indigenous groups may not do any better than others at protecting and sustainably developing their land and natural resources. Given the opportunity to share in the profits, the Kayapó allowed gold miners and loggers to plunder their territory for several years. Other indigenous groups have made similar deals with predatory outsiders in exchange for short-term gain. They seek medical services, schools, access roads, electricity, clean water and other necessities, and if the government does not fulfill its legal responsibility to provide these things, they may turn to private companies for them. The experience of the Kayapó and other groups shows that selling off resources may bring immediate benefits, but the long-term damage caused by logging, mining and other industrial extractive activities harms people's health and the environment. To ensure a prosperous future in a relatively unspoiled environment, indigenous peoples need incentives to stop selling off their natural patrimony, as well as workable development plans and support to carry them out.

The Scientific Case for Indigenous Rights

Recent scientific research indicates that tropical deforestation is one of several causes of global climate change, which may have devastating effects around the world.[3] Indigenous efforts to use the environment sustainably (and thereby reduce or slow global climate change) deserve support, not only for their sake but for ours. Northern donations and tax monies back the private, governmental and intergovernmental programs that finance these initiatives. That makes every taxpayer a funder who needs to know how his or her money is being spent and to what end. Stockholders in corporations that invest in projects affecting indigenous people also need to know the results of their investments. According to our legal and moral codes, if we take resources (whether mahogany, natural gas, diamonds or tropical fruit) from other people, we owe them equitable compensation in return. We have no rights to steal from anyone.

In all these ways Northerners are involved in and responsible for what happens to indigenous people and are therefore accountable to them. Whether or not we think about them as we drink coffee from areas indigenous people have lost to invaders, or as we drive cars powered by petroleum extracted from indigenous lands in Mexico, Ecuador or Venezuela, they are certainly affected by our consumption patterns. And all human beings share an interest in the future of the earth, our only home.

If we allow indigenous people to disappear, abetting the process of extinction by investing in projects that ruin their environment, we lose the promise of diversity. As Darwin pointed out, "during the modification of the descendants of any one species, and during the incessant struggle of all species to increase in numbers, the more diversified the descendants become, the better will be their chance of success in the battle for life" (Darwin 1963: 125).

According to paleontologist Rick Potts, humans evolved in response to extremely unstable climatic and environmental conditions. "Human adaptation to novel contingencies ... means that our unique social behaviors, mental capacities and ecological strategies are not attached to strict limits defined in our past." As a species we have an enviable flexibility. "The strange buoyancy of the hominids is in us, a hopeful heritage of response to novel environmental dilemmas" (Potts 1996: 277).

Most modern societies, however, see themselves in opposition to, separate from and outside nature, conceived of as an unchanging obstacle to human dominion, something to be conquered, exploited and controlled. Many members of these societies take a short-term view of human actions, unable to imagine consequences beyond their lifetime. Yet, under the impact of human activity, things seem to be changing almost too quickly to cope with. Evolutionary change takes place over thousands of generations, but in a few generations we seem to have altered fundamentally our relationship to nature. In contrast, indigenous peoples represent a less destructive form of adaptation that increasingly seems like an Eden we cannot return to.

Human beings still comprise an extremely diverse species, thanks to our highly developed capacity for learning from the particular experiences of our ancestors and passing along cultural knowledge to our descendants. Depending on local conditions, human populations have created myriad ways of adapting to or even altering and controlling their surroundings. Northerners tend to consider their technological domination of the environment as evidence of superiority over people with simpler ways of life. I daresay we would have considerable difficulty adapting to the Kayapó or Yanomami environment if we were suddenly deprived of our material aids, however. And since evolution is an open-ended process, we cannot know what parts of our species will be most successful in the long run. Modern civilisation could be a mere "flash in the pan," to be remembered as we recall the vanished glories of the Inca or Mycenae. Or it could become a monumental catastrophe, if the changes we have set in motion have unintended consequences that turn out to be overwhelmingly destructive or unsustainable. We indulge in a self-serving illusion if we think that the short-lived success of civilisation constitutes evidence of "natural selection." [4]

Anthropologist Adam Kuper can summon only guarded optimism about our species' prospects:

This changing, growing, converging world we now live in is the long-term product of the cumulative and accelerating development of culture, which began only some 40 millennia ago ... And yet it is not easy to be sanguine about our future. Human beings have been their own worst enemies ... but it is not too optimistic to believe we have the means to survive, and perhaps to make things better. (Kuper 1994: 244)

Potts emphasises, "We are part of nature's ongoing process," and thus dependent on it. Whatever we do to it, we do to ourselves.

As civilisation's creations and customs spread throughout the world and overwhelm local forms, diversity – whether cultural or biological – suffers. What looks in the short term like a successful adaptation may be the harbinger of decline. A few varieties of hybrid seeds crowd out the many local forms that could give rise to robust new varieties. Disease bacteria may become resistant to lifesaving drugs faster than we can develop new cures. Babies die because their mothers give them infant formula mixed with contaminated water, instead of breastfeeding them. When we neglect, scorn or do away with local variations in culture, no matter how remote or "primitive" they seem, we may deprive our own descendants of options for a good life.

Indigenous people can teach us much about what is useful. They also have an intrinsic right to live that does not depend on what they can teach us. In defending their rights, we exercise and uphold our own. Despite the commonness of selfish, corrupt and immoral acts among human beings, we can still hold on to a sense of our species' common good and act upon it.

When human populations were small and isolated from one another, living off the land by hunting and gathering, they often applied the idea of the common good only to themselves and their relatives. Groups like the Yanomami and the Kayapó did not define others, who spoke different languages and followed different customs, as fully human. Although our species' social universe has expanded geometrically during the past 10,000 years, to include billions instead of dozens or hundreds of others, we still have difficulty in comprehending others' humanity. Unlike some species, we carry on a high level of internecine conflict.[5] Especially during the past 10,000 years, we have destroyed as much as we have created.

At the same time, we depend on human beings thousands of miles away from us, to supply us with the materials we need to construct and maintain our extremely elaborate way of life. Many denizens of civilisation work long hours to create tangible and intangible goods and the means to transport them to people they never see or know. We have created extraordinarily complex social, economic and political arrangements that link us to other humans in myriad ways. This economic and political interdependence affects people, animals and habitats in the remotest corners of the world. We can use our unparalleled learning and teaching capabilities to transcend both our biological limitations and the unintended consequences of our inventiveness, but we are neither omniscient nor omnipotent. Rushing along the edge of a precipice, we seem to pay scant attention to the faraway consequences of our actions until it is almost too late. Humans are "too clever by half."

Seeking More than Mere Survival

After oil has spilled or mercury has entered the food chain, indigenous and other traditional groups are often left to cope with the consequences of outside impingements. But that is not all they have to do. They also struggle to sustain themselves, preserve their traditions and benefit from the changes that have come unbidden to them. Their response to the outside world has been not only to redefine their identity but also to organise to protect their interests. Community, regional, national and international movements founded and run by indigenous people now defend indigenous rights. For example, in Brazil, CIR (Indigenous Council of Roraima) defends the interests of the Macuxi and neighboring groups in the northern Amazon. CAPOIB (Council for Articulation of Indigenous Peoples and Organisations in Brazil) has its headquarters in Brasilia and an indigenous staff that represents indigenous interests before Congress and government agencies. Indian organisations in all eight Amazon basin nations have banded together with international NGOs in the Coalition for Amazonian Peoples and their Environment, whose headquarters are in Washington, DC.

Allied organisations offer these groups financial and moral support. The Indian Law Resource Center (ILRC) of Washington, DC, started providing legal help to the Yanomami in 1978. Since then the Center has gone to the Inter-American Commission of Human Rights, the United Nations Commission on Human Rights and UN Working Group on Indigenous Populations, among other intergovernmental bodies, on the Yanomami's behalf. In 1989–90, when genocide was raging, ILRC appealed for UN Secretary General Perez de Cuellar's intervention. In April 1991 the Center arranged for Davi Yanomami to meet with Perez de Cuellar as well as US State Department, World Bank and Inter-American Commission officials. Brazil's President responded to the international pressure by ordering expulsion of the garimpeiros and ratifying the demarcation of the Yanomami reserve.

Alliances between the people on the ground and sympathisers far away are not easy to establish or maintain, but they have become necessary vehicles for indigenous self-preservation. A Washington office with a long e-mail list, or a well-timed letter to a Congress member, can sometimes accomplish as much as a group of warriors burning electrical transmission towers. The warriors may gain more attention at first, but their political allies may work for years to secure long-term benefits in the world capitals where policy makers make the decisions that determine their fate.

For the most part, indigenous people gain little attention from Northern media or policy makers, and Brazil disappears from the international news for months at a time, except when a massacre or scandal hits the headlines. Since the 1993 Haximu massacre, the Yanomami have received little media coverage. Once Payakan fell from grace, the Kayapó ceased being symbols of ecological wisdom and largely disappeared from public view. In general, feature stories about Indians tend to focus on bad news. A few headlines prove the point: "Rape by Decree" (*Guardian*), "Decree Endangers Survival of Brazilian Indians" (*Christian Science Monitor*), "Indians of Brazil Live 5.6 Years Less" (*Folha de São Paulo*). Even the positive headlines are qualified by pessimism: "For Once, a Victory for Indians" (*The Washington Post*), "Latin American Indians Organise to Improve Lives Even Worse than in US" (*The New York Times*). It is not surprising, then, that many people think of Indians as pathetic remnants of once-great cultures, soon to disappear forever.

And yet the Indians continue fighting to survive. Despite grim predictions of extinction, their persistence in following their traditions testifies to their "fitness" for what Darwin called "the battle for life." A man of his time, Darwin expressed repulsion at the "savage who delights to torture his enemies, offers up bloody sacrifices, practices infanticide without remorse, treats his wives like slaves, knows no decency, and is haunted by the grossest superstitions" (1981: 404–5). Montaigne or Léry might have used these same phrases to describe Europeans at many moments in their bloody history.

Adam Kuper observed that the inhabitants of Tierra del Fuego, to whom Darwin was referring in this passage:

... would have been ... appalled to learn that the Anglo-Saxons had the effrontery to claim kinship to them, yet nevertheless practised slavery and mechanised warfare, flogged women in public, sent their children away from home in early childhood, and believed that their god had been born to a virgin. (Kuper 1994: 62)

Yet Darwin managed to transcend his Victorian prejudices when he contemplated the grandeur of life on earth, in which "endless forms most beautiful and most wonderful have been and are being evolved." He also recognised that creation can grow out of destruction. "Each at some period of its life, during some season of the year, during each generation or at intervals, has to struggle for life and to suffer great destruction," he wrote. "The vigorous, the healthy and the happy survive and multiply" (Darwin 1963: 462). Indigenous ways of life have thrived during most of the 2-million-year history of our species. Five-hundred years of assaults upon them by what we call civilisation may amount to but a season of destruction. Their fate, and ours, is still in the making.

It is poignant now to remember Davi Yanomami's sad instructions to Bruce Albert, "Tell them ... how we were, how we had good health, how we weren't dying so much, we didn't have malaria. Tell how ... we hunted, how we held feasts, how happy we were." In contrast, the sight of the Kayapó in fighting gear, dancing in front of the Brazilian Congress to defend their interests, exhilarates. "I have never taken so much pleasure," Léry wrote, "as I delighted then in seeing those savages do battle." Unlike Léry's Tupinambá, the Kayapó use their fearsome reputation to gain their objectives mostly without bloodshed, by fighting their battles ritualistically. They and the Yanomami have learned difficult but valuable lessons through experience, and they are changing in order to survive. So must we. Only time – and the countless acts and events that constitute cultural and biological evolution – will tell who is most fit, and for what.

Notes

Chapter 1 Setting the Scene

1. According to the Brazilian Constitution of 1988 (my translation):

   > Lands traditionally occupied by the Indians are reserved for their permanent possession, and the exclusive use of the riches of the soil, the rivers and the lakes existing on them falls to them ... Acts with the object of occupation, control and possession of lands referred to in this article, or exploitation of the natural riches of the soil, rivers and lakes are null and void and without juridical effect ...

   To indigenous advocates, this provision makes Decree 1775/96 unconstitutional.
2. In September 1997 an association of retired military officers challenged the constitutionality of the Yanomami demarcation in Brazil's Supreme Court (CIMI 1997c). This was one among many attempts to overturn this demarcation that did not succeed.

Chapter 2 In Search of the Other

1. Caminha quotations translated by Linda Rabben.
2. In the mid-fifteenth century, Pope Nicholas V gave the kings of Portugal and Spain "full and free permission to invade, search out, capture and subjugate enemies of Christ wherever they may be and to reduce their persons into perpetual slavery." This authorisation was extended from Africa to the Americas in 1493.
3. Villas Boas quotations translated by Linda Rabben.
4. The neighboring Juruna called the Kayapó "wooden lips" because the men wore wood plates in their lower lips. Few do today.
5. Anthropologist Dominique Gallois, who studies the Waiapi Indians of Amapá state, has criticised FUNAI's continued use of the "attraction" method to make contact with "isolated" Indians. She believes it establishes an unhealthy relationship of domination and dependence (Grupioni 1994: 121–34).
6. At the beginning of the twentieth century, about 300 indigenous groups lived in Brazil. By the end of the century, about 200,

137

speaking 180 languages, survived. Most groups have fewer than 1,000 members.

7. According to the tax records of the Yanomamö Survival Fund, which are available for public inspection according to US law, the Fund has been inactive since at least 1993. I found no record of either the Yanomamö Survival Fund or the American Friends of Venezuelan Indians having supported development or relief projects for the Yanomami or other indigenous groups. A written request to Chagnon for information in mid-1997 went unanswered.

8. Michael Heckenberger's archeological research in the Xingu region in 1996 uncovered earthworks dating from 1350–1450 AD, and he concluded that Amazonian indigenous groups were making war upon one another well before contact with Europeans started. Xingu is far from Yanomami territory, but such evidence may affect future theorising on the causes of indigenous bellicosity. On the other hand, Brian Ferguson, who studies war cross-culturally, says that earthworks could be for flood control and not defensive purposes.

9. Chagnon hated this analysis. In his 1996 review, he commented, "Ferguson comes uncomfortably close to claiming that my presence among the Yanomamö, especially between 1964 and 1970, 'caused' the wars I described ... Ferguson adds machetes to his argument as a material supplement to my vileness and trading caprice" (Chagnon 1996: 671).

10. Bruce Albert (1997b) contends:

> Yanomami warmaking cannot be reduced to a matter of contact and access to tools (just as it cannot be reduced to any other purely material cause, whether proteins or genes). These factors can certainly affect the intensity of warfare (in the sense of raiding), but the fact remains that Yanomami warfare (as a system of values and a ritual-political device) is above all part of a complex social totality, outside of which it cannot be understood.

Chapter 3 The People from Between the Waters

1. The Kayapó call themselves Mebengokre, the people from between the waters; indigenous enemies gave them the derisive name "Kayapó," which means "monkey-like."

Chapter 4 Payakan: A Cautionary Tale

1. In June 1997 the Xavante stopped one of the federal government's new mega-projects, the Araguaia–Tocantins–Rio das

Mortes Waterway, by obtaining (with the help of ISA) an injunction from a federal judge.

> The decision of the judge was based on the fact that an environmental license had not been granted by IBAMA to carry out the work on the waterway and that the constitutional demand that the construction of such waterways passing through indigenous areas must be authorized by the National Congress after it has consulted the communities concerned, was not adhered to. Two Xavante communities of approximately 1,600 people live near the proposed route of the waterway in the municipalities of Água Boa and Nova Xavantina. (SEJUP 1997c)

2. A Kayapó leader threatened to sue the Body Shop in 1996, accusing the firm of using his image for commercial purposes without compensating him.

Chapter 5 Yanomami Apocalypse

1. The Brazilian government offered to sell the world's largest niobium deposit to private buyers in 1997 for a mere US $600,000. "The low price is due to two factors: the world market is oversupplied with the product and the area where the deposit is located [a national park and a state bio-reserve near Yanomami territory] is difficult to reach" (Figueiredo 1997: 3). The welfare of indigenous groups living near the niobium deposit apparently was not taken into consideration. However, IBAMA, the federal environmental protection agency, sought to stop the sale on the grounds that it would be unconstitutional. This is an example of how conflicting policies and mandates lead Brazilian government agencies to work against one another.
2. In the mid-1990s CEDI merged with NDI to become ISA.
3. Yanomami leaders from Brazil and Venezuela met for the first time in late 1997. They expressed strong opposition to mining and proposed mega-projects that threaten their communities and environment (CCPY 1997 *Update*).

Chapter 6 Davi

1. In this interview, Davi refers to Xawara as feminine, while on other occasions he identifies it as masculine.
2. Quotations from Albert (1991) translated by Linda Rabben.
3. For a description of Salesian missionary schools in Venezuela for the Yanomami, see Salomone (1997: 89–106).

Chapter 7 Fit for What?

1. According to a 1996 report by the World Wildlife Fund, the proportion of the earth covered by forests has dropped from 40 per cent to 26 per cent since the Industrial Revolution. The most rapid and sustained destruction has occurred since 1950. About 15 million hectares of tropical forests disappear each year. During the 1980s, Brazil and Indonesia accounted for 45 per cent of the global loss. Since the 1992 Earth Summit, forest destruction in Brazil and other countries has increased substantially.
2. The UN's Draft Declaration on the Rights of Indigenous Peoples, which has been in the works for more than a decade, goes even further in specifying the responsibilities of governments to protect indigenous land, cultural, political, labor and other rights.
3. Although consensus has not been reached, most climatologists agree that the heating of the earth's atmosphere, due to human activities producing increasing emissions of carbon dioxide, may lead to flooding, droughts and other damaging events around the world. People living in deforested areas in Brazil have noticed local climate changes that make their subsistence more difficult.
4. Stephen Jay Gould (1997a: 35) insists that "selection cannot suffice as a full explanation for many aspects of evolution ... in domains both far above and far below the traditional Darwinian locus of the organism." Like many anthropologists, Gould believes that "the passage of acquired traits to subsequent generations," or cultural evolution, supersedes much slower Darwinian evolution among humans. As geneticist Steve Jones (1997: 41) puts it: "Our evolution is unique in that it is mainly in the mind."
5. In their provocatively titled book, *Demonic Males*, Richard Wrangham and Dale Peterson (1996: 251) suggest that humans can reduce their violence, which seems to have reached a terrifying level across the species, by reducing the dominance of males over females. "Male demonism is not inevitable. Its expression has evolved in other animals, it varies across human societies, and it has changed in history ... We can have no idea how far the wave of history may sweep us from our rougher past."

Bibliography

Abreu, João Batista de. 1996. "Ingleses acusados de enganar os caiapós," *Jornal do Brasil* (Rio de Janeiro), 23 February: 7.

Ação pela Cidadania. 1989. "Roraima, Brazil: A Death Warning," *Cultural Survival Quarterly* 13(4): 59–67.

Agência Ecumênica de Notícias. 1993. "Commitment of Brazilian Authorities to Uphold Rights of Indigenous People Called into Question by AI," 21 January. São Paulo, Brazil.

Albert, Bruce. 1989. "Yanomami 'Violence': Inclusive Fitness or Ethnographer's Representation," *Current Anthropology* 30(5): 637–40.

—— 1991. "Xawara: O ouro canibal e a queda do céu," in *Povos Indígenas no Brasil 1987/88/89/90*. São Paulo: Centro Ecumênico de Documentação e Informação.

—— 1993. "O massacre dos Yanomami de Haximu," on ax.brasil computer conference, 7 October.

—— 1995. "O ouro canibal e a queda do céu: uma crítica xamânica da economia política da natureza," *Série Antropologia No. 174*. Brasilia: Universidade de Brasilia.

—— 1996. "O massacre dos Yanomami de Haximu," in C.A. Ricardo (ed.), *Povos Indígenas no Brasil 1991/1995*. São Paulo: Instituto Sócioambiental.

—— 1997a. "'Ethnographic Situation' and Ethnic Movements," *Critique of Anthropology* 17(1): 53–65.

—— 1997b. Personal communication.

Alcântara, Euripedes. 1995. "Índio também é gente," *Veja* (São Paulo, Brazil), 6 December: 7–10.

Alencar, José de. 1975. *Iracema, Lenda do Ceará*. Rio de Janeiro: Livraria Francisco Alves Editora.

Alonso, George. 1995. "Disputa deixa índios morrerem sem assistência," *Estado de São Paulo*, 13 November.

American Anthropological Association. 1991. "Report of the Special Commission to Investigate the Situation of the Brazilian Yanomami." Arlington, VA.

Amerindian Peoples Association. 1997. "Region 9 Amerindians Form Regional Council to Oppose Mining Concessions and to Demand Full Recognition of their Land Rights." Press release on Amazon Coalition listserve, 2 November. Georgetown, Guyana.

AMIGRANSA. 1997. "Decision de la corte suprema de justicia sobre mineria en Imataca," Amazon Coalition listserve, 12–14 November.

Amnesty International. 1992. "Brazil. We Are the Land. Indigenous Peoples' Struggle for Human Rights." London: AI.
—— 1993. "A Shameful Legacy. Human Rights Violations against the World's Indigenous Peoples," *Focus*, May: 3–6.
—— 1997. "Statement by Amnesty International on the Occasion of the World Bank/International Monetary Fund Annual Meetings, Hong Kong, September 1997." London.
Anaya, S. James. 1994. "International Law and Indigenous Peoples, Historical Stands and Contemporary Developments," *Cultural Survival Quarterly*, Spring: 42–4.
Andersen, Martin E. 1994. "Turning our Backs on Those who Were Here First?" *The Washington Times*, 24 November: A17.
Associação Vida e Ambiente. 1994. "Plano de ações para a elaboração de propostas para as áreas indígenas – Baú/Mekragnoti." Brasilia, Brazil.
—— 1995a. *Boletim da AVA* 1(2).
—— 1995b. "Relatório sobre o momento Kayapó e perspectivas." Brasilia, Brazil.
—— 1995c. "Subsídios para discussão sobre projetos alternativos para as áreas Mebengokre." Brasilia, Brazil.
Barsh, Russel L. 1994. "Making the Most of ILO Convention 169," *Cultural Survival Quarterly* 18(1): 45–7.
Berwick, Dennison. 1992. *Savages. The Life and Killing of the Yanomami*. London: Hutchinson.
Biocca, Ettore. 1970. *Yanoáma. The Story of Helena Valero, a Girl Kidnapped by Amazonian Indians*. New York: Dutton.
"Biografia, Megaron Txucarramãe." n.d.
Braga, Teodomiro. 1991. "Cresce chance de ajuda americana a Amazônia," *Jornal do Brasil*, 5 December.
Brasil, Amazonas. 1995. "Violência contra a soberania nacional. Tentativas de internacionalização da Amazônia," *O Diário* (Boa Vista), 23 December: B1.
The Brasilians. 1997. "Calls for Adoption of a Declaration to Protect the Rights of Indigenous People," January: 5E.
Brasiliense, Ronaldo. 1993. "Complô armado. Sydney Possuelo atribuí sua queda da Presidência da Funai a pressões militares e econômicas e a intrigas palacianas," *IstoÉ*, May. São Paulo, Brazil.
—— 1995. "Caiapós endividados tomam posto da Funai," *Correio Braziliense*, 15 November.
Brazil Network (UK). 1992–7. *Newsletter*. London.
Brazilian Embassy (Washington, DC). 1993. "Brazilian Policy on Indigenous Population," *Current Issues* 3.
Brooke, James. 1990. "Rain Forest Indians Hold Off Threat of Change," *The New York Times*, 3 December: A4.
—— 1993a. "Brazil Is Evicting Miners in Amazon," *The New York Times*, 8 March: A7.
—— 1993b. "Gold Miners and Indians: Brazil's Frontier View," *The New York Times*, 7 September: A4.
—— 1993c. "Crackdowns on Miners Follow Indian Killings," *The New York Times*, 19 September: 10.

—— 1995a. "Amazon Indians' Battle for Land Grows Violent," *The New York Times*, 11 June: 3.

—— 1995b. "Atrocity Case in Amazon Is Botched," *The New York Times*, 29 June: A6.

—— 1995c. "Asphalt Ribbon Binds Brazil and Venezuela," *The New York Times*, 24 September: 11.

—— 1995d. "Proposed Cuts in Indian Programs Hit Those Who Rely Most on Federal Aid," *The New York Times*, 15 October: 16.

Buchanan, Rob. 1993. "The Rain Forest Rape," *Details*, March: 46–56, 214.

Burns, E. Bradford. 1993. *A History of Brazil* (third edition). New York: Oxford University Press.

Caminha, Pero Vaz de. 1974. "Carta," in C.L. Hulet (ed.), *Brazilian Literature 1*. Washington, DC: Georgetown University Press.

Campanha pela Demarcação das Terras Indígenas na Amazônia. 1992. "Índios mudam estratégia e lançam campanha publicitária." São Paulo, Brazil.

CCPY (Comissão pela Criação do Parque Yanomami). 1989–97. *Update*. São Paulo, Brazil.

—— 1993. *Urihi* 16 (March).

—— 1995. "The Survival of the Yanomami," *Yanomami Urgente*, 17 April.

CEDI (Centro Ecumênico de Documentação e Informação). 1991. *Povos Indígenas no Brasil 1987/88/89/90*. São Paulo.

Centeno, Júlio César. 1997. "The Management of Corruption in Venezuela," on Amazon Coalition listserve, 5 June.

Center for the Study of Human Rights. 1992. *Twenty-Four Human Rights Documents*. New York: Columbia University.

CESR, Oxfam America, Rainforest Action Network. 1996. "Oil in the Rainforest. The Impacts of the Responses to Texaco's Operations in the Ecuadorian Amazon."

Chagnon, Napoleon A. 1983. *Yanomamö. The Fierce People* (third edition). New York: CBS College Publishing.

—— 1988. "Life Histories, Blood Revenge and Warfare in a Tribal Population," *Science* 239: 985–92.

—— 1990. "On Yanomamö Violence: Reply to Albert," *Current Anthropology* 31(1): 49–52.

—— 1992. *Yanomamö, the Last Days of Eden*. New York: Harcourt Brace Javonovich.

—— 1995. "L'Ethnologie du déshonneur: brief response to Lizot," *American Ethnologist* 22: 187–9.

—— 1996. "Review of *Yanomami Warfare*," *American Anthropologist* 98(3): 670–2.

Chernela, Janet. 1988. "Potential Impacts of a Proposed Amazon Hydropower Project," *Cultural Survival Quarterly* 12(2): 20–3.

—— 1997. "Blood, Gold and Histories, as They Flow in the Northwest Amazon of Brazil," paper delivered at American Anthropological Association annual meeting, November.

CIMI (Conselho Indigenista Missionário). 1987. "Doctrine of National Security Threatens Brazil's Indians," *Cultural Survival Quarterly* 11(2): 63–5.

—— 1993a. "Madeireiras apressam a retirada de mogno de área indígena," on ax.brasil computer conference, 10 October.

—— 1993b. "Governo brasileiro permite que militares interfiram na demarcação das terras indígenas," on ax.brasil computer conference, 28 October.

—— 1993c. "Pelo menos 42 índios foram assassinados no Brasil em 1993," on ax.brasil computer conference, 23 December.

—— 1994a. *1993: A Violência contra os Povos Indígenas no Brasil.* Brasilia: Conferência Nacional dos Bispos Brasileiros.

—— 1994b. "Exploração de madeira provoca danos aos povos indígenas," on ax.brasil computer conference, 14 January.

—— 1994c. "Índios yanomami no Brasil são prostituidas em troca de comida," on ax.brasil computer conference, 19 September.

—— 1994d. "Índios kayapó expulsam 2000 garimpeiros de suas terras," on ax.brasil computer conference, 22 September.

—— 1995. "Organizações indígenas – um novo sujeito político," on brasil.noticias computer conference, 4 May.

—— 1996a. "Yanomami em assembléia chamam FHC e o Ministro Jobim de medrosos e irresponsáveis," on ax.brasil computer conference, 18 January.

—— 1996b. "Povo tembé: uma história que é o retrato da situação dos 350 mil índios no país," *Porantim*, June–July: 7–10.

—— 1996c. "Condenados cinco acusados do massacre yanomami," on ax.brasil computer conference, 20 December.

—— 1996d. "Army and Funai Accused of Helping to Decimate the Yanomami," Amazon Coalition listserve, 23 December.

—— 1997a. "Índios reagem ao descaso do governo federal," on ax.brasil computer conference, 17 February.

—— 1997b. "Áreas indígenas são alvo das empresas madeireiras internacionais," on ax.brasil computer conference, 20 June.

—— 1997c. "The Military Bring Suit against Yanomami Area," *CIMI Newsletter 281*, on ax.brasil computer conference, 10 October.

—— 1997d. "Mais uma operação para retirada de garimpeiros na área yanomami," on ax.brasil computer conference, 27 November.

—— 1997e. "Invasions of Indigenous Lands in 1996 Confirm Denunciations," CIMI listserve, 5 December.

Cipola, Ari. 1996. "Índios do Brasil vivem 5,6 anos menos," *Folha de São Paulo*, 7 June: 8.

Clay, Jason. n.d. [1991]. "Resource Wars: Nation and State Conflicts of the Twentieth Century," unpublished ms.

Coalition for Amazonian Peoples and Their Environment. 1996. "Annual Meeting Report, June 26–July 1, Quito, Ecuador." Washington, DC.

Colchester, Marcus and Fiona Watson. 1995. "Venezuela: Violations of Indigenous Rights. Report to the International Labour Office on the Observation of ILO Convention 107." London.

Conklin, Beth A. and Laura R. Graham. 1995. "The Shifting Middle Ground: Amazonian Indians and Eco-Politics," *American Anthropologist* 97(4): 695–710.

Conselho Indígena de Roraima. 1994. "Situação fundiária das terras indígenas de Roraima." Boa Vista, Roraima, Brazil.
—— 1995. "Relação dos inquéritos policiais que apuram crimes praticados contra ou entre índios em Roraima, 1991 a 1994."
Correio Braziliense. 1995. "Edital de leilão judicial juízo federal da terceira vara," 21 May: 39.
Coulter, Robert T. 1994. "The Draft Declaration on the Rights of Indigenous Peoples: What Is It? What Does It Mean?" Washington, DC: Indian Law Resource Center.
Cox, Larry. 1991. Letter to the Editor, *The Brasilians* (New York), December.
Cristaldo, Janer. (1995). "Uma teocracia na Amazônia," *Folha de São Paulo,* 12 February: B1.
CSL Films. 1996. *Warriors of the Amazon* (television documentary), Chris Curling, producer.
Cubel, Katia. 1993. "Garimpeiro também é vítima, diz ministro," *Folha de São Paulo,* 20 August.
Cultural Survival Quarterly. 1989. "The Kayapó Bring Their Case to the United States," 13(1): 18–19.
—— 1996. "Genes, People and Property," Special Issue, 20(2).
Daes, Erica-Irene. 1994. "Introductory Statement on the United Nations Draft Declaration on the Rights of Indigenous Peoples, Working Group on Indigenous Populations, Subcommittee on Prevention of Discrimination and Protection of Minorities, 46th Session, 22 August." Geneva: United Nations.
—— 1996. "Introductory Statement. 14th Session of the Working Group on Indigenous Populations, 29 August." Geneva: United Nations.
Darwin, Charles. 1963. *The Origin of Species.* New York: Dutton.
—— 1981. *The Descent of Man, and Selection in Relation to Sex.* Princeton, NJ: Princeton University Press.
Davis, Shelton. 1977. *Victims of the Miracle. Development and the Indians of Brazil.* New York: Cambridge University Press.
Distrito Sanitário Yanomami. 1991. "Primeiro Relatório do Distrito Sanitário Yanomami." Boa Vista: Fundação Nacional de Saúde.
Durning, Alan. 1991. "Native Americans Stand Their Ground," *World Watch,* November–December: 10–17.
Eakin, Marshall C. 1997. *Brazil: The Once and Future Country.* New York: St Martin's Press.
The Earth Times. 1997. "Rainforest Roads: A 'Compound Disaster,'" 16–30 April: 11.
Environmental News Service. 1997. "Nature's Services Worth Trillions, Scientists Told," on Ecological Enterprises listserve, 17 February.
Epstein, Jack. 1996. "Decree Endangers Survival of Brazilian Indians," *Christian Science Monitor,* 7 March: 6.
Escobar, Gabriel. 1996a. "Indians of Ecuador Coalescing in Quest for Political Power," *The Washington Post,* 23 July: A12.
—— 1996b. "For Once, a Victory for Indians," *The Washington Post,* 24 September: A13.

Estado de São Paulo. 1993. "Conselho nacional da Amazônia é instalado," 4 December.

Estanislau, Maria. "Funcionários da Funai são mantidos como reféns no Pará," *Folha de São Paulo,* 15 November.

Farnsworth, Clyde. 1997. "Australians Resist Facing Up to Legacy of Parting Aborigines from Families," *The New York Times,* 8 June: 18.

Feeney, Patricia. 1997. "Dehumanizing Growth. The Cost of Brazil's Stabilization: Eroding Indians' Rights." Oxford: Oxfam United Kingdom and Ireland.

Feijó, Atenéia and Marcos Terena. 1994. *O Índio Aviador.* São Paulo: Editora Moderna.

Ferguson, R. Brian. 1995. *Yanomami Warfare. A Political History.* Santa Fe, NM: School of American Research.

Ferrer, Yadira. 1997. "Suicide Threat by Indigenous Group," InterPress Service, on ips.english computer conference, 19 June.

Figueiredo, Lucas. 1997. "Ibama quer impedir venda de jazida no AM," *Folha de São Paulo,* 7 October.

Fisher, William H. 1991. "The Institutional Roots of Indigenous Environmental Protest: The Kayapó and Macrodevelopment in Pará, Brazil," unpublished ms.

—— 1994. "Megadevelopment, Environmentalism and Resistance: The Institutional Context of Kayapó Indigenous Politics in Central Brazil," *Human Organization* 53(3): 220–32.

—— 1995. "Kayapó Social Organization and the Central Brazilian Frontier: Dualism and Authority," paper delivered at the Latin American Studies Association meeting, 28–30 September.

FMV (Fundação Mata Virgem). 1990. "Unified Health Care Program in Xingu National Park." Brasilia, Brazil.

—— 1991. Untitled memo on sterilization of Payakan's wife, Irekran.

—— n.d. [1992]. "Terms of Reference for Getting Intruders Out of Kayapó, Mekragnotire and Baú Indian Areas."

—— n.d. [1992]. "Background Information – Menkragnoti Indigenous Area."

—— n.d. [1992]. "Program for Scholastic Education in the Xingu Indian Park."

—— 1992. *Folha da Mata Virgem.* May.

—— 1993. "Third and Final Operational Report on Demarcation of the Menkragnoti Indian Area," 16 November.

—— 1993. "Texto a ser proferido pelo líder indígena Megaron Txucarramãe em audiência pública do Congresso dos Estados Unidos da América," July.

—— 1993. "Spring Expedition Trip to Menkragnoti Area," November.

—— 1994a. "ONG exige indenização para kayapós contaminados por mercúrio," March.

—— 1994b. "Plano de ação imediata para a área menkragnoti (PAI)," April.

—— 1995. *Relatório de Atividades 1989–1994.*

Folha de Boa Vista. 1997. "Projeto que permite mineração será votado na próxima semana," 22 August.

Folha de São Paulo. 1991a. "Autor de 'Raoni' processa dois brasileiros," 21 November: 12.

—— 1991b. "Retrato falado: Sting," 8 December.

—— 1992. "Começa este mês demarcação do maior território do país," 5 July: 15.

—— 1995. "Começa hoje nova retirada de garimpeiros," 5 June.

FUNAI (Fundação Nacional do Índio). 1994. "Termo de referência para desintrusão das áreas indígenas Kayapó, Menkragnoti e Baú." Brasilia, Brazil.

—— 1995. "Informação No. 007/CPTI/DPI." Brasilia, Brazil.

Gabeira, Fernando. 1991a. "Brasil discute com G7 verbas para preservar a Amazônia," *Folha de São Paulo*, 7 December.

—— 1991b. "G7 concede US $250 mil a projeto-piloto para Amazônia," *Folha de São Paulo*, 9 December.

Galé, Nelino. 1997. "Agrava-se a situação na área yanomami," CIMI listserve, 29 July.

Galvão, Eduardo. 1967. "Indigenous Cultural Areas of Brazil, 1900–1959," in J. Hopper (ed.), *Indians of Brazil in the Twentieth Century*. Washington, DC: Institute for Cross-Cultural Research.

Gay, Kathlyn. 1993. *Rainforests of the World*. Santa Barbara, CA: ABC-CLIO.

Gazeta Mercantil (São Paulo). 1994. "Proibida exploração de madeira em área indígena," on brasil.noticias computer conference, 9 April.

Goering, Laurie. 1996. "Rain Forest Residents Sue Texaco," *The Washington Post*, 16 July: A16.

Gomes, Laurentino. 1992. "A cegueira verde. Movidos pelo fanatismo, os ecoxiitas recusam as evidências de que Paiakan é culpado de estupro," *Veja* (São Paulo), 17 June: 82–4.

Gomes, Laurentino and Paulo Silber. 1992. "A explosão do instinto selvagem. Paiakan, o cacique-simbolo da pureza ecológica, estupra e tortura uma adolescente," *Veja* (São Paulo), 10 June: 68–73.

Gomes, Severo. 1990. *No Meio do Caminho*. Brasilia: Centro Gráfico do Senado Federal.

Gomez, Gale Goodwin. 1997a. "The Impact of Gold Mining on Yanomami Health," paper delivered at American Anthropological Association annual meeting, November.

—— 1997b. Personal communication.

Gonçalves, Francisco. 1994. "Garimpeiros invadem a reserva ianomami," *Jornal do Brasil*, 9 August.

Gould, Stephen Jay. 1997a. "Darwinian Fundamentalism," *New York Review of Books* 44(10): 34–7.

—— 1997b. "Evolution: The Pleasures of Pluralism," *New York Review of Books* 44(11): 47–52.

Gross, Daniel. 1996. "The World Bank in Brazil," *Anthropology Newsletter* 37(5): 2.

Grupioni, Luís Donisete Benzi, ed. 1994. *Índios no Brasil*. Brasilia: Ministério da Educação e do Desporto.

Guardian (London). 1997. "New Hope for Forests. But the Chainsaw May Win in the End," 10 March.

Gutkowski, Cris. 1994. "Paulinho Paiakan é absolvido," "Polícia temia conflito se houvesse condenação," "Justica absolve Paiakan de estupro," *Folha de São Paulo*, 29 November: B1.

Hamilton, Dominic. 1997. "Pemon Indians Paralyze Powerlines," EnviroNews Service on hr.indigenous computer conference, 4 June.

Hemming, John. 1978. *Red Gold. The Conquest of the Brazilian Indians*. Cambridge, MA: Harvard University Press.

—— 1987. *Amazon Frontier. The Defeat of the Brazilian Indians*. London: Macmillan.

ILRC (Indian Law Resource Center). 1990. "Statement to Inter-American Commission on Human Rights on Case #7615: Violations of the Human Rights of the Yanomami Indians." Washington, DC.

INESC (Instituto dos Estudos Sócio-Econômicos). 1994. "Yanomami: os limites da cidadania," *Informativo*, No. 50: 10. Brasilia.

International Labour Office. 1991. *Convention No. 169. Convention Concerning Indigenous and Tribal Peoples in Independent Countries*. Geneva: United Nations.

InterPress Service. 1993. "Yanomami Massacre Becomes National Security Issue," on ips.english computer conference, 27 August.

—— 1994. "Estudios muestran contaminacion de indigenas con mercurio," on ips.espanol computer conference, 26 July.

—— 1997a. "Caldera y Cardoso vuelven a verse," on ips.espanol computer conference, 5 April.

—— 1997b. "Presencia de 3.000 'garimpeiros' amenaza a yanomamis," on ips.espanol computer conference, 16 August.

—— 1997c. "Violencia contra indigenas en aumento, segun Iglesia," on brasil.noticias computer conference, 5 December.

ISA (Instituto Sócioambiental). 1995. "Xicrin rompem com modelo predatório e defendem manejo sustentável," on ax.brasil computer conference, 13 June.

—— 1996–7. *Parabólicas*. São Paulo.

—— 1997. "FHC homologa 22 terras indigenas," electronic mail, 6 November.

Johnson George. 1996. "Dispute over Indian Casinos in New Mexico Produces Quandary on Law and Politics," *The New York Times*, 18 August: 24.

Johnston, Barbara R., ed. 1997. *Life and Death Matters. Human Rights and the Environment at the End of the Millennium*. Walnut Creek, CA: Alta Mira Press.

Jones, Steve. 1997. "Go Milk a Fruit Bat!" *New York Review of Books* 44(12): 38–41.

Jornal do Brasil (Rio). 1991a. "Fazendeiro não deixa índio assumir reserva," 19 November.

—— 1991b. "Collor demarca área indígena com 9,4 milhoes de hectares," 29 November.

—— 1991c. "Exercito e Ibama vão impedir garimpo no Pico da Neblina," 29 November.

—— 1991d. "Mata Virgem ajudará demarcação," 30 November.

—— 1993. "Ricúpero buscará recursos externos para a Amazônia," on brasil.noticias computer conference, 10 September.

Jornal do Comércio (Rio). 1993. "Militares povoarão a Amazônia," on brasil.noticias computer conference, 6 October.

Kayapó, A'Kjabor, *et al.* 1993. Letter to AIMEX [Associação Exportadoras da Madeira do Estado do Pará], 17 May.

Klintowitz, Jaime. 1995. "A culpa é do índio," *Veja* (São Paulo), 20 September: 66–8.

Kuper, Adam. 1994. *The Chosen Primate. Human Nature and Cultural Diversity*. Cambridge, MA: Harvard University Press.

Leão, Eduardo. 1994a. "Garimpeiros são expulsos por kayapó," *Porantim*, September: 15.

—— 1994b. "Mercúrio contamina kayapó," *Porantim*, October: 13.

Leary, Warren E. 1992. "Explorers of Amazon Branch Retrace Roosevelt Expedition," *The New York Times*, 10 April: A12.

Leitão, Ana Valéria Nascimento Araújo. 1994. "Indigenous Peoples in Brazil," *Cultural Survival Quarterly*, Spring: 48–50.

Léry, Jean de. 1990. *History of a Voyage to the Land of Brazil, Otherwise Called America*, trans. Janet Whatley. Berkeley: University of California Press.

Lévi-Strauss, Claude. 1967. *Tristes Tropiques*. New York: Atheneum.

Lewan, Todd. 1997. "Brazil Shifts Use of Foreign Funds to Restore Native Atlantic Glory," *The Washington Times*, 17 March: A12.

Lewis, John. 1990. "Non-Governmental Organizations and International Human Rights," *New York Law Journal* 203(71): 1, 4.

Lizot, Jacques. 1985. *Tales of the Yanomami. Daily Life in the Venezuelan Forest*. Cambridge: Cambridge University Press.

—— 1994. "On Warfare: An Answer to N.A. Chagnon," *American Ethnologist* 21(4): 845–62.

—— 1996. E-mail communication on Yanomami health problems in Venezuela, 6 December.

Machado, Marina. 1993. "The Health Situation of the Kubenkokre and Pukanu Tribes." New York: Rainforest Foundation International.

MacMillan, Gordon. 1995. *At the End of the Rainbow? Gold, Land and People in the Brazilian Amazon*. New York: Columbia University Press.

Magalhães, Edgard D. 1995. "Breve notícia e relato histórico da situação sanitária e violência contra as populações indígenas de Roraima: em especial o caso Yanomami." Boa Vista: DSY/FNS.

—— 1996. "Memorando," "Saúde Yanomami – 1995."

Martins, Américo. 1993. "Comandante diz que reserva é ameaça ao país," *Folha de São Paulo*, 20 August.

McIntyre, Loren. 1991. *Amazonia. Photographs and Text*. San Francisco: Sierra Club Books.

Medeiros, Alexandre. 1995. "Amazônia em dois tempos/2," *Jornal do Brasil – Domingo*, 29 October: 75–85.

Melloni, Eugenio. 1997. "Xingu Dam Plan to Be Revived," *Gazeta Mercantil*, 31 March, on hr.indigenous computer conference, 11 April (trans. Glenn Switkes).

Michaels, Julia. 1992. "Rape Trial Highlights Brazilian Native Rights," *Christian Science Monitor*, 19 June: 6.
Ministério Público. 1992. "Laudos periciais, Silvia Letícia da Luz Ferreira." Belém: Estado do Pará.
Mongiano, Aldo. 1995. Letter to Fernando Henrique Cardoso, President of Brazil, 23 August.
Montaigne, Michel. 1984. *Essays*. New York: Penguin.
Monteiro, Joaquim. 1995. "Mogno roubado dos caiapós vai a leilão," *Correio Braziliense*, 30 May: 4.
Moreira, Memélia. 1991. "A estratégia do genocídio yanomami," "Cronologia de um genocídio documentado," in CEDI, *Povos Indígenas no Brasil 1987/88/89/90*, 162–4, 172–93.
NACLA Report on the Americas. 1996. "Gaining Ground. The Indigenous Movement in Latin America," 29(5): 14–43.
—— 1997. "The Body Shop Controversy" (Letter of Adrian Hodges and reply of Jan Rocha), 30(4): 4.
Nash, Nathaniel. 1992. "Latin American Indians: Old Ills, New Politics," *The New York Times*, 24 August: 1, A6.
NDI (Núcleo de Direito Indígena). 1994. "Relatório de viagem, área indígena kayapó," "Comunidades indígenas conseguem importantes vitórias na defesa de suas terras," *Informativo*, March–April: 3–4.
Nepstad, Daniel and Eric Davidson. 1993. "'Deforestation's Other Side' Isn't Rosy," Letter to the Editor, *The Washington Post*, 8 October: A26.
O'Connor, Geoffrey. 1993. Unpublished interview with Sting.
Oliveira, Claudio Esteves and Deise Alves Francisco. 1994. *Report on Health Activities in the Yanomami Area*. Boa Vista: CCPY.
—— 1996. *Relatorio de Atividades de Saúde na Área Yanomami*. São Paulo: CCPY.
Oliveira, Edmundo. 1991. *A Vitimização dos Índios na Amazônia*. Belém: CEJUP.
Oliveira, Luíz Rodrigues de. 1995. "Mudanças no decreto 22/91 ameaçam PP-G7," *Jornal do Brasil*, 2 March: 4.
Onis, Juan de. 1992. *The Green Cathedral. Sustainable Development of Amazonia*. New York: Oxford University Press.
Paiakan, Paulinho. n.d. "Project proposal. Aukre Village, Kayapó Nation, Brazil."
Pereira, Euclides. 1994. "Roraima: um estado de violência institucionalizada." Boa Vista: CIR.
Peters, John F. 1997. "Health Care and the Problem of Miners among the Yanomami on the Mucajaí River in Brazil," paper delivered at American Anthropological Association annual meeting, November.
Pietricovsky, Iara, Ricardo Verdum, *et al.* 1995. *Mapa da Fome entre os Povos Indígenas no Brasil (II)*. Brasilia: INESC/PETI-MN/ANAI-BA.
Pinagé, Luíz Carlos. 1991. "The Current Status of Development and Environment – Brazil," paper presented at International Forum on Sustainable Development.
Pisani, Elizabeth. 1991. "Opposition Mounts to the New Yanomami Reserve," *Guardian*, 27 December: 26.

Plant, Roger. 1991. "Land Rights for Indigenous and Tribal Peoples in Developing Countries," World Employment Programme Working Paper. Geneva: ILO.

Podesta, Don. 1993. "Efforts to Save Rain Forests Raise Suspicions in Brazil," *The Washington Post*, 11 October: 1, 23.

Porantim. 1992. "Caso Paiakan. Não foi julgado mas já é culpado," June: 6.

—— 1992. "A morte do coronel kayapó," July–August: 13.

Posey, Darrell A. 1995. "Sustainable Characteristics of Kayapó Society," paper presented at LASA meeting, September.

Potts, Rick. 1996. *Humanity's Descent. The Consequences of Ecological Instability*. New York: William Morrow.

Priest, Dana. 1996. "American Radar Aiding Drug Fight," *The Washington Post*, 7 January: A22.

Rabben, Linda. 1988. "Land, Debt and Democracy," *The Nation*, 30 April: 597–601.

—— 1990. "Brazil's Military Stakes Its Claim," *The Nation*, 12 March: 341–2.

—— 1992a. "Notes on Demarcation Procedures." New York: Rainforest Foundation International.

—— 1992b. "Memo on Payakan." New York: Rainforest Foundation International.

—— 1993. "Demarcation – And Then What?" *Cultural Survival Quarterly*, Summer: 12–14.

—— 1995. "Kayapó Choices: Short-Term Gain vs. Long-Term Damage," *Cultural Survival Quarterly*, Summer: 11–13.

Rainforest Foundation International. 1991. "The Rainforest Foundation and Fundação Mata Virgem Urge Pres. Collor to Demarcate All Indian Territories as Foundation Releases First Annual Report." New York.

—— 1992a. "Jungle Operation Begins Demarcation," 21 August. New York.

—— 1992b. "Mercury Project at SBPC," 25 August. New York.

—— 1992c. "News Update," Winter. New York.

—— n.d. [1992] "Mekragnoti Indigenous Area – Background." New York.

—— 1993, 1994. *Quarterly Journal* (New York).

—— 1996. *Out of the Forest* (newsletter), Summer. New York.

Rainforest Foundation United Kingdom. 1995. *Annual Report 1994–95*. London.

Ramos, Alcida Rita. n.d. [1988?]. "Área indígena yanomami," unpublished ms.

—— 1990a. "Indigenismo de Resultados," *Série Antropologia 100*. Brasilia: Universidade de Brasilia.

—— 1990b. "Ethnology Brazilian Style," *Cultural Anthropology* 5(4): 452–72.

—— 1991. "Os direitos do índio no Brasil. Na encruzilhada da cidadania," *Série Antropologia 116*. Brasilia: Universidade de Brasilia.

—— 1992. "Sobre la utilidad social del conocimiento antropologico," *Antropologicas*, July: 51–9.

—— 1994. "The Hyperreal Indian," *Critique of Anthropology* 14(2): 153–71.

—— 1995a. "A profecia de um boato," *Série Antropologia 188*. Brasilia: Universidade de Brasilia.

—— 1995b. "Por falar em paraíso terrestre," *Série Antropologia 191*. Brasilia: Universidade de Brasilia.

—— 1995c. *Sanumá Memories. Yanomami Ethnography in Times of Crisis*. Madison: University of Wisconsin Press.

—— 1995d. "Seduced and Abandoned: The Taming of Brazilian Indians," in V.R. Dominguez and C.M. Lewis, (eds), *Questioning Otherness. An Interdisciplinary Exchange*. Iowa City, IA: Center for International and Comparative Studies, University of Iowa.

Reuters. 1997. "Church Says Brazilian Indians under Attack by Whites," on Ecological Enterprises listserve, 13 March.

Ribeiro, Berta. 1990. *Amazônia Urgente. Cinco Séculos De História e Ecologia*. Belo Horizonte: Itataia.

Ribeiro, Darcy. 1967. "Indigenous Cultures and Languages of Brazil," in J. Hopper (ed.), *Indians of Brazil in the Twentieth Century*. Washington, DC: Institute for Cross-Cultural Research.

Ricardo, Carlos Alberto, ed. 1996. *Povos Indígenas no Brasil 1991/1995*. São Paulo: Instituto Socioambiental.

Ricardo, Fany and Marcio Santilli. 1997. *Terras Indígenas no Brasil: Um Balanço da Era Jobim*. São Paulo: Instituto Socioambiental.

Robbins, Jim. 1997. "For Indians, Environment Becomes New Battleground," *The New York Times*, 9 February: 32.

Roberts, David. "The Suya Sing and Dance and Fight for a Culture in Peril," *Smithsonian* 27, May: 63–75.

Rocha, Jan. 1991. "Prospectors Bring Malaria back to Brazil's Indians," *Guardian*, 7 July: 10.

—— 1996a. "Rape by Decree," *Guardian*, 31 January.

—— 1996b. "Burning Ambition," *Guardian*, 20 November.

—— 1997. "Influx of Asian Timber Giants Threatens Efforts to Manage Rain Forest," *The Washington Times*, 17 March: A12.

Roque, Atila, *et al.* n.d. [1996]. "Social Watch: Brazil. Poverty Again at the Center of Debate," on www.chasque.apc.org/socwatch/generbra.html. Rio: FASE/IBASE.

Rousseau, Jean-Jacques. 1950. "A Discourse on the Origin of Inequality," in *The Social Contract and Discourses*. London: Dent.

Saffirio, John and Raymond Hames. 1983. "The Impact of Contact: Two Yanomami Case Studies. The Forest and the Highway," *Cultural Survival Occasional Paper 11*, November.

Sagoff, Mark. 1997. "Do We Consume Too Much?" *The Atlantic*, June: 80–96.

Salamone, Frank A. 1997. *The Yanomami and their Interpreters. Fierce People or Fierce Interpreters?* Lanham, MD: University Press of America.

Saldanha, Patrícia. 1992. "FNS abandona sanitaristas na selva," *Porantim*, June: 5.

Saldanha, Patrícia and Eduardo Leão. 1992. "Eco-92 garante a demarcação," *Porantim*, June: 4.

Schemo, Diana Jean. 1995a. "Hope for Amazon Rain Forest: New Fruit," *The New York Times*, 24 September: 12.

—— 1995b. "Amazon Is Burning Again, as Furiously as Ever," *The New York Times*, 12 October: A3.

—— 1996a. "In Brazil, Indians Call on Spirits to Save Land," *The New York Times*, 21 July: 1, 6.

—— 1996b. "Indians in Brazil Wither in an Epidemic of Suicide," *The New York Times*, 25 August: 1, 6.

—— 1996c. "Brazil Indefinitely Postpones Ruling on Indian Land Claims," *The New York Times*, 11 October: A5.

—— 1996d. "Legally, Now, Venezuela to Mine Fragile Lands," *The New York Times*, 8 December: 1, 22.

Schmink, Marianne and Charles H. Wood. 1992. *Contested Frontiers in Amazonia*. New York: Columbia University Press.

Schomberg, William. 1996. "Brazil Wins Funding for Amazonian Highway," *The Washington Times*, 14 September.

Schwartzman, Stephan. 1986. "World Bank Holds Funds for Development Project in Brazil," *Cultural Survival Quarterly* 10(1): 25–7.

—— 1997. "Fires in the Amazon: An Analysis of NOAA-12 Satellite Data 1996–1997." Washington, DC: Environmental Defense Fund listserve, 1 December.

SEJUP (Serviço Brasileiro de Justiça e Paz). 1994. "Foreign Minister asked German Embassy to Omit Demarcation Funding from Programa Piloto Grant," *News from Brazil*, on sejup.news computer conference, 24 March.

—— 1996. "Gold Prospectors Return to Indigenous Area," *News from Brazil*, on sejup.news computer conference, 22 August.

—— 1997a. "Indians Regroup in a Shantytown in São Paulo," *News from Brazil*, on sejup.news computer conference, 5 March.

—— 1997b. "Indigenous Lands Bargained for Votes in Favour of Reelection," *News from Brazil*, on sejup.news computer conference, 22 May.

—— 1997c. "Work on Waterway Halted by Court Order," *News from Brazil*, on sejup.news computer conference, 26 June.

Smole, William J. 1976. *The Yanoama Indians. A Cultural Geography*. Austin, TX: University of Texas Press.

Soltani, Atossa and Tracey Osborne. 1997. *Arteries for Global Trade, Consequences for Amazonia*. Malibu, CA: Amazon Watch.

Sponsel, Leslie. 1992. "Amazonia as an Ecosystem: General Overview," paper presented at "Transforming the Amazonian Rain Forest" symposium, March.

—— 1994a. "The Killing Fields of the Brazilian and Venezuelan Amazon: The Continuing Destruction of the Yanomami and Their Eco-Systems by Illegal Gold Miners, Future Scenarios and Actions," paper presented at American Anthropological Association annual meeting, December.

—— 1994b. "The Yanomami Holocaust Continues," in B.R. Johnston (ed.), *Who Pays the Price? The Sociocultural Context of Environmental Crisis*. Washington, DC: Island Press.

—— 1997. "The Master Thief: Human and Environmental Impacts and Rights in Relation to Gold Mining and Mercury Contamination in the Amazon," in B.R. Johnston (ed.), *Life and Death Matters*. Walnut Creek, CA: Alta Mira Press.

Stavenhagen, Rodolfo. 1996. "Indigenous Rights: Some Conceptual Problems," in Elizabeth Jelin and Eric Hershberg (eds), *Constructing Democracy. Human Rights, Citizenship and Society in Latin America*. Boulder, CO: Westview Press.

Storto, Luciana. n.d. "A Report on Language Endangerment in Brazil," unpublished ms.

Survival International. 1992. *Indians of the Americas. Invaded but not Conquered*. London.

Switkes, Glenn. 1997. "Victory! Judge Halts Dam on Indian Land," on ax.brasil computer conference, 29 March.

Tanaka, Nair. 1994. "Health Trip to Mekragnoti," New York: Rainforest Foundation International.

Tullberg, Steven M. 1994. "Indigenous Peoples, Self-Determination and the Unfounded Fear of Secession," unpublished ms. Washington, DC: Indian Law Resource Center.

—— 1996. "Statement on Behalf of the Indian Law Resource Center by Steven M. Tullberg to the Briefing of the Congressional Human Rights Caucus on Brazil's Decree 1775/96."

Turner, Terence. 1978. "The Txukahamãe Kayapó Are Alive and Well in the Upper Xingu," *Survival International Review* 3(2): 18–21.

—— 1988. "History, Myth and Social Consciousness among the Kayapó of Central Brazil," in J. Hill (ed.), *Rethinking History and Myth*. Urbana: University of Illinois Press.

—— n.d. [1989]. "Five Days at Altamira," Kayapó Support Group.

—— 1990. Unpublished ms (later published as Turner 1993).

—— 1991a. *The Mebengokre Kayapó*, unpublished ms.

—— 1991b. "Representing, Resisting, Rethinking. Historical Transformations of Kayapó Culture and Anthropological Consciousness," in G.W. Stocking, Jr. (ed.), *Colonial Situations. Essays on the Contextualization of Ethnographic Knowledge*. Madison, WI: University of Wisconsin Press.

—— 1991c. "Death and Democracy in Brazil," *The New York Times*, 18 June: A21.

—— 1992a. "Os Mebengokre Kayapó: história e mudança social," in M. Carneiro da Cunha (ed.), *Historia dos Indios no Brasil*. São Paulo: Secretaria Municipal de Cultura.

—— 1992b. "Viagem aos Kayapó, 11–24 julho 1992." São Paulo: ISA.

—— 1993. "Role of Indigenous Peoples in the Environmental Crisis: The Case of the Brazilian Kayapó," *Perspectives in Biology and Medicine*, 36 (3): 526–45.

—— 1994. "The Yanomami: Truth and Consequences," *Anthropology Newsletter*, May: 46, 48.

—— 1995a. "A Sociedade Kayapó." São Paulo: ISA.

—— 1995b. "An Indigenous People's Struggle for Socially Equitable and Ecologically Sustainable Production: The Kayapó Revolt against Extractivism," *Journal of Latin American Anthropology*, n.s. 1 (1): 98–121.

—— 1996a. "Brazil: Indigenous Rights vs. Neoliberalism," *Dissent*, Summer: 67–9.

—— 1996b. "Association Protests Threat to Indigenous Land Rights," *Anthropology Newsletter* 37(5): 22.

—— 1997. "Mineral Extraction by and for Indigenous Amazonian Communities: Gold Mining by the Waiapi and Kayapó," paper delivered at American Anthropological Association annual meeting, November.

—— In press. "Indigenous Rights, Environmental Protection and the Struggle over Forest Resources in the Amazon: The Case of the Brazilian Kayapó," in J. Conway, K. Keniston and Leo Marx (eds), *Earth, Air, Fire and Water*. Cambridge, MA: MIT Press.

—— and Davi Kopenawa Yanomami. 1991. "I Fight Because I Am Alive," *Cultural Survival Quarterly*, Summer: 59–64.

US Department of State. 1997. "1996 Human Rights Report: Brazil," Washington, DC: Bureau of Democracy, Human Rights and Labor.

Verdum, Ricardo. 1994. "A fome e os povos indígenas: luzes no fim do túnel," *Informativo*, No. 53: 10. Brasilia: INESC.

Verswijver, Gustaaf. 1978. "Séparations et migrations des Mekragnoti, groupe Kayapó du Brésil Central," *Société Suisse des Américanistes, Bulletin* 42: 47–59.

Viana, Virgílio, Isabelle Gianini, *et al.* 1994. "Plano diretor da reserva Kayapó-Xicrin do Cateté." São Paulo: ISA.

Villas-Boas, André. 1993. *"Green Gold" on Indian Land. Logging Company Activities on Indigenous Land in the Brazilian Amazon*. São Paulo: CEDI.

Villas-Boas, Orlando and Claudio. 1994. *A Marcha para o Oeste. A Epopéia da Expedição Roncador-Xingu* (fourth edition). Rio: Editora Globo.

Wallace, Scott. 1993. "Rape and Politics in the Rain Forest," *Penthouse*, November.

Warrick, Joby. 1997. "Checkup Time for the Environment," *The Washington Post*, 22 June: A6.

Werner, Dennis, *et al.* 1979. "Subsistence Productivity and Hunting Effort in Native South America," *Human Ecology* 7(4): 303–15.

—— 1982. "Variation in Swidden Practices in Four Central Brazilian Indian Societies," *Human Ecology* 10(2): 203–17.

Wiggins, Armstrong. 1990. "Violations of the Human Rights of the Yanomami Indians. Statement of the Indian Law Resource Center, September 28, 1990, Case No. 7615, Inter-American Commission on Human Rights," Washington, DC: ILRC.

Wilford, John Noble. 1991. "Oldest Pottery in Americas Is Found in Amazon Basin," *The New York Times*, 13 December.

Wilson, Richard A. 1997. "Human Rights, Culture and Context: An Introduction," in R.A. Wilson (ed.), *Human Rights, Culture and Context, Anthropological Perspectives*. London: Pluto Press.

World Conference of Indigenous Peoples on Territory, Environment and Development. 1992. "Kari-Oca Village Declaration." Rio.

World Rainforest Movement. 1997. "Brazil: Tupinikim and Guarani indigenous peoples vs. Aracruz Cellulose," *Bulletin*, on WRM list-serve, 3 June.

Wrangham, Richard and Dale Peterson. 1996. *Demonic Males. Apes and the Origins of Human Madness.* Boston, MA: Houghton Mifflin.

Yanomami, Davi Kopenawa. 1989. "Letter to All the Peoples of the Earth," *Cultural Survival Quarterly* 13(4): 68–9.

Zacquini, Carlo. 1993. "Yanomami Air Strip is Inaugurated on Mayday," CCPY *Update* 66, 3 May.

Index